WISDOM THROUGH THE AGES

ITALIAN AND ENGLISH
PROVERBS AND QUOTATIONS

LA SAGGEZZA ATTRAVERSO I SECOLI

PROVERBI E CITAZIONI
ITALIANI E INGLESI

Pasquale Varano

WISDOM THROUGH THE AGES

ITALIAN AND ENGLISH
PROVERBS AND QUOTATIONS

LEGAS

Library of Congress Cataloging-in-Publication Data

Wisdom through the ages : Italian and English proverbs and quotations / Pasquale Varano.
    p. cm.
English and Italian.
Includes index.
ISBN 1-881901-44-0 (alk. paper)
1. Quotations, English. 2. Quotations, Italian. 3. Quotations, Italian—Translations into English. I. Varano, Pasquale, 1927-
   PN6080.W58 2004
   082—dc22

                       2004026005

Printed and bound in Canada

For information and for orders, write to:

Legas

P.O. Box 149
Mineola, New York 11501
USA

3 Wood Aster Bay
Ottawa, Ontario
K2R 1D3 Canada

www.legaspublishing.com

Dedico questo libro
alla memoria di mia madre e di mio padre,
a mia moglie Clara
e ai nostri figli
Sal Mario, Rose Ann and Susann

II savio ... crescerà in dottrina,
e l'intelligente acquisterà sagacia
per capire i proverbi e le allegorie,
i detti del savi e i loro enimmi.

La Sacra Bibbia, Antico Testamento: Proverbi, 1:5-6.
Edizioni Paoline

A wise man ... will increase learning; and a man
of understanding shall attain unto wise counsels:
To understand a proverb, and the interpretation;
the words of the wise, and their dark sayings.

The Holy Bible, Old Testament: Proverbs. 1:5-6.
King James version

SOMMARIO - CONTENTS

PREFAZIONE

LA SAGGEZZA ATTRAVERSO I SECOLI è in parte, il patrimonio della saggezza e dell'esperienza dei nostri antenati. Questi gioielli linguistici, portatori della sapienza dei nostri avi, sono illustrati e commentati con proverbi e citazioni tematicamente paralleli di autori classici e moderni che abbracciano un periodo di oltre due millenni - da Omero a oggi. Lo scopo di questo libro bilingue e multiculturale è di offrire una singolare raccolta di proverbi scelti che rispecchiano principalmente alcuni aspetti della cultura e della civiltà italiana e anglosassone.

L'ortografia originale di alcune parole è stata modernizzata tranne in casi di riferimenti classici e biblici. Tutti i proverbi italiani e inglesi sono presentati nella loro forma originale. In casi rari, però, dove il corrispondente proverbio inglese manca oppure dove la ricerca dell'autore non è riuscita ad individuarne uno, la traduzione in inglese è presentata tra parentesi. Inoltre, tutte le citazioni italiane sono accompagnate da una traduzione in inglese.

Per facilitarne l'uso, questa raccolta è ripartita in quattro parti: Ordinamento tematico; Indice dei proverbi italiani; Indice dei proverbi inglesi; Indice degli autori.

PARTE PRIMA - Dodici capitoli tematici.

Ciascun capitolo si concentra su un aspetto universale della vita: amore, felicità, destino, morte. Ogni proverbio è numerato e le corrispondenti citazioni illustrative sono disposte in ordine cronologico discendente allo scopo di mettere in rilievo lo sviluppo e la cristallizzazione del proverbio nella sua forma attuale. Le citazioni danno il nome dell'autore, il titolo dell'opera, il capitolo, il verso e la data, o se la citazione è presa da un'opera drammatica, il nome dell'autore, il titolo dell'opera, l'atto, la scena, il verso, e la data.

PARTE SECONDA - Indice dei proverbi italiani.

PARTE TERZA - Indice dei proverbi inglesi.

Sia i proverbi italiani che quelli inglesi sono disposti in ordine alfabetico. Ciascun proverbio in ambo le lingue è numerato per facilitarne la ricerca nei capitoli tematici.

PARTE QUARTA - Indice degli autori.

Gli autori e i loro pseudonimi sono elencati in ordine alfabetico con le date di nascita e di morte. Il numero di ogni chiamata indica la rispettiva chiamata dell'autore nei capitoli tematici.

Pasquale Varano

PREFACE

WISDOM THROUGH THE AGES is, in part, the patrimony of our forefathers' wisdom and experience. These linguistic jewels, carriers of the wisdom of our forebears, are illustrated and commented with thematically parallel proverbs and quotations of classical and modern authors spanning a period of more than two millennia - from Homer to the present day. The purpose of this bilingual, multicultural book is to provide a unique collection of selected proverbs that chiefly reflect certain facets of Italian and Anglo-Saxon culture and civilization.

The original spelling of certain words has been modernized except for classical and biblical references. All Italian and English proverbs are presented in their original form. In rare cases, however, where the corresponding English proverb is missing or where the author's research failed to locate one, an English translation is provided in parentheses. Also, all Italian quotations are accompanied by a corresponding English translation.

To facilitate its use, this collection is divided into four parts: Topical arrangement; Index of Italian proverbs; Index of English proverbs; Index of authors.

PART I - Twelve topical chapters.

Each chapter focuses on a universal aspect of life: love, happiness, destiny, death. Each proverb is numbered and its corresponding illustrative quotations are arranged in a descending chronological order to show the development and crystallization of the proverb in its present form. Quotations give author, title of the work, chapter, verse and date, or if the quotation is from a dramatic work, author, title of the work, act, scene, line, and date.

PART I I - Index of Italian proverbs.

PART II I - Index of English proverbs

Both the Italian and English proverbs are listed in alphabetical order. Each proverb in both languages is numbered to facilitate its location in the topical chapters.

PART IV - Index of authors.

Authors, and their pseudonyms, are listed alphabetically with their dates of birth and death. Entry numbers indicate the author's entries in the topical chapters.

Pasquale Varano

1. Amor ha fatto diventare uomini savi, pazzi; uomini dotti, ignoranti;uomini forti, deboli.

> John Florio, *Firste Fruites.* (1578)

Love has made wise men become fools, learned men ignorant, strong men weak.

> Florio, *ibid.*

*To be wise and love

Is hardly granted to the gods above.

> John Dryden, *Palamon and Arcite,* bk. II, 1. 364.(1680)

* To be wise and love,

Exceeds man's might; that dwells with gods above.

> Shakespeare, *Troilus and Cressida,* act III, sc. ii, l. 163. (1601)

* To love and be wise is hardly granted to a god

> Publilius Syrus, *Sententiae.* (c. 43 B.C.)

2. In guerra, nella caccia e negli amori, per un piacer mille dolori.

War, hunting, and love, have a thousand troubles for their pleasure.

> Thomas Fuller, *Gnomologia.* (1732)

* Hunting, hawking, paramours, for one joy a thousand displeasures.

> A Scottish proverb

* War; hunting, and love, are as full of troubles as of pleasure.

> An English proverb

* Hunting, hawking and love, for one joy have a hundred griefs.

> John Ray, *English Proverbs.* (1678)

* In war, hunting, and love, men for one pleasure a thousand griefs prove.

> George Herbert, *Jacula Prudentum.* (1640)

3. Occhio che non vede, cuore che non desidera.

* *Se l'occhio non mira, il cuor non sospira.*

(What the eye does not see, the heart does not desire).

* We cannot wish for what we do not know.

> Voltaire (François Marie Arouet), Zaire, act I, sc. i. (1730)

* What the eye views not, the heart craves not.

> William Penn, *No Cross. No Crown,* ch. 5. (1669)

* The heart dreams not of what the eye sees not.
> Miguel de Cervantes, *Don Quixote de la Mancha,* pt. II, ch. 67. (1615) Shelton, tr.

* The jewel that we find, we stoop and take't,

Because we see it, but what we do not see

We tread upon, and never think of it.
> Shakespeare, *Measure for Measure,* act II, sc. i. 1. 24. (1604)

* [There is] no desire for the unknown.
> Ovid, *Ars Amatoria,* bk. III, 1. 397. (c. 1 B.C.)

4. Occhio non vede, cuore non duole.

What the eye doesn't see, the heart doesn't grieve over.
> An English proverb

* What the eye does not see, the heart does not rue.
> Richard Chenevix Trench, *On the Lessons in Proverbs,* ch. 6. (1853)

* When the eye sees what it never saw, the heart will think what it never thought.
> Thomas Fuller, *Gnomologia.* (1732)

* The present eye praises the present object.
> Shakespeare, *Troilus and Cressida,* act III, sc. iii, l.180. (1601)

* What the eye sees not, the heart rues not.
> John Heywood, *Proverbs,* pt. II, ch. 7. (1546)

5. L'occhio vuole la sua parte.

The eye will have his part.
> George Herbert, *Jacula Prudentum.* (1640)

* For I just can't make my eyes behave,

Two bad brown eyes, I am their slave;

My lips may say, "Run away from me,"

But my eyes say, "Come and play with me."
> Will D. Cobb, *I Just Can't Make My Eyes Behave.*(1906)

6. L'occhio attira l'amore.

The eye lets in love.
> An English proverb

* Love comes in at the eye.
> William Butler Yeats, *A Drinking Song.* (1910)

* Loving comes by looking.

John Clarke, *Paroemiologia*. (1639)

* From women's eyes this doctrine I derive:

They are the ground, the books, the academes

From whence doth spring the true Promethean fire.

Shakespeare, *Love's Labour's Lost,* act IV, sc. iii, 1. 302. (1595)

* The eyes start love.

Publilius Syrus, *Sententiae.* (c. 43 B.C.)

The eyes, like sentinels have the highest station.

Cicero, *De Natura Deorum,* bk. II, ch. 56, sec. 140. (c. 45 B.C.)

7. *Dov'è l'amore, là è l'occhio.*

* *Dov'è l'amore, l'occhio corre.* (Toscano)

(Where love is, there the eye is).

Love's tongue is in the eyes.

Phineas Fletcher, *Piscatorie Eglogues,* canto V, stanza 12. (1771 edition)

* The heart's letter is read in the eyes.

George Herbert, *Jacula Prudentum.* (1640)

* The eyes have one language everywhere.

George Herbert, *Jacula Prudentum.* (1640)

* In the forehead and the eye, the lecture of the heart is read.

Thomas Draxe, *Bibliotheca.* (1616)

* There are often voice and words in a silent look.

'Ovid, *Ars Amatoria,* bk. I, 1. 574. (c. 1 B.C.)

8. *Amor solo d'amor si pasce.*

(Love feeds only on love).

Lovers live by love.

John Ray, *English Proverbs.* (1670) John Heywood, *Proverbs,* pt. I, ch. 10. (1546)

* The dessert of love is ... love.

George Pettie, *Petite Pallace,* p. 17. (1576)

* Love itself is the chief nourishment of love.

Propertius, *Elegies,* bk. III, elegy 21, 1.4. (c. 22 B.C.)

9. *Amor con amor si paga.*

Love is love's reward.

John Dryden, *Palamon and Arcite,* bk. II, 1. 373. (1680)

* Love makes love.

> Robert Stephen Hawker, *Footprints of Former Men in Far Cornwall,* p. 77. (1870)

* Love and be loved.

> Benjamin Franklin, *Poor Richard's Almanack.* (1756)

* Love begets love, then never be

Unsoft to him who's smooth to thee.

> Robert Herrick, *Love Looks for Love.* (1648)

* Love goes toward love.

> Shakespeare, *Romeo and Juliet,* act II, sc. ii, 1. 156. (1595)

* Show your love to win love.

> Alexander Barclay, *The Mirrour of Good Manners,* p. 74. (c. 1510)

10. *Amor è il vero prezzo con cui si compra amore.*

> * *Amor non si compra né si vende;*

ma in premio d'amor amor si rende.

Love is the true price of love.

> George Herbert, *Jacula Prudentum.* (1640)

* Love can neither be bought or sold; its only price is love.

> Henry George Bohn, *Handbook of Proverbs.* (1855)

* Love's the coin to market with for love.

> James Sheridan Knowles, *The Love-Chase,* act I,sc. ii. (1837)

* The only present love demands is love.

> John Gay, *The Espousal,* 1. 56. (c. 1732)

* Love looks for love.

> Robert Herrick, *Love Looks for Love.* (1648) John Clarke, *Paroemiologia.* (1639)

* Love is not found in the market.

> George Herbert, *Jacula Prudentum.* (1640)

* All for love, and nothing for reward.

> Edmund Spenser, *The Faerie Queene,* bk. II, canto, viii, stanza 2. (1590)

11. *Amore è cieco.*

> * *Amor è cieco, ma vede da lontano.*

Love is blind.

> Shakespeare, *The Two Gentlemen of Verona,* act II, sc. i, 1. 76. (1594)
> Geoffrey Chaucer, *The Canterbury Tales: The Merchant's Tale,* 1.

354.

(c. 1387) Plautus, *Miles Gloriosus,* 1. 1260. (c. 200 B.C.)

* The eye is the index of the mind.

A Latin proverb

* The eye looks, but it is the mind that sees.

Edward White, *Life in Christ,* bk. IV, ch. 25. (1875)

* I have heard of reasons manifold

Why Love must needs be blind,

But this the best of all I hold

His eyes are in his mind.

Samuel Taylor Coleridge, *Reason for Love's Blindness.* (1828)

* Though Love is blind, yet 'tis not for want of eyes.

Thomas Fuller, *Gnomologia.* (1732)

* Love looks not with the eyes, but with the mind,

And therefore is wing'd Cupid painted blind.

Shakespeare, *A Midsummer-Night's Dream,* act I, sc. i, 1. 234. (1596)

12. Chi ama, teme.

(He who loves, fears).

Love is full of fear.

The Oxford Dictionary of English Proverbs. (1948)

* Where love is great, the littlest doubts are fear;

When little fears grow great, great love grows there.

Shakespeare, *Hamlet,* act III, sc. ii, 1. 183 (1600)

* Fie, fie, fond love, thou art so full of fear.

Shakespeare, *Venus and Adonis,* 1. 1021. (1593)

* True love is never without fear.

François Rabelais, *Gargantua and Pantagruel,* bk. III, ch. 18. (1545)

* Love is a thing filled with anxious fear.

Ovid, *Heroides:* Epistle i, 1. 12. (c. 10 B.C.)

13. Non è amore senza gelosia.

*   *Amor dà per mercede gelosia e rotta fede.*

Love is never without jealousy.

James Kelly, *Scottish Proverbs.* (1721)

There can never be love without it [jealousy].

Theodore Edward Hook, *Jack Brag,* ch. 3. (1837) ,

* The reward of love is jealousy.

 Thomas Fuller, *Gnomologia*. (1732)

* Jealousy is always born together with love.

 La Rochefoucauld, *Maxims:* maxim 361 (1665)

* Love, thou know'st, is full of jealousy.

 Shakespeare, *The Two Gentlemen of Verona,* act II, sc. iv, 1. 178. (1594)

* Jealousy is grounded upon love.

 George Pettie, *Petite Pallace,* p. 102. (1576)

14. Amore non è senza amaro.

 * *Dov'è grand'amore, quivi è gran dolore.*

 (Love is not without bitterness).

 Love is a bitter-sweet.

  The Oxford Dictionary of English Proverbs. (1948)

 All that we know in love is bitter.

  Conrad Potter Aiken, *Annihilation*, stanza 8.(c. 1936)

 * It [love] is to be all made of sighs and tears.

  Shakespeare, *As You Like It,* act V, sc. ii, 1. 90. (1600)

 * Love is a fiend, a fire, a heaven, a hell,

 Where pleasure, pain, and sad repentance dwell.

  Richard Barnfield, *The Shepherd's Content,* stanza 38. (1595)

15. Grand'amore, gran dolore.

  John Florio, *Firste Fruites.* (1578)

 Great love, great sorrow.

  Florio, *ibid.*

 * There are as many sorrows in love as shells on the shore.

  Ovid, *Ars Amatoria,* bk. II, 1. 519. (c. 1 B.C.)

 In love, pain and pleasure are always at war.

  Publilius Syrus, *Sententiae.* (c. 4.3 B.C.)

16. L'amore è amaro, ma rinfranca il cuore. (Siciliano)

 (Love is bitter, but it invigorates the heart).

 Love is a sweet tyranny, because the lover

 endures his torments willingly.

  Henry George Bohn, *Handbook of Proverbs.* (1855)

 * Pains of love be sweeter far

Than all other pleasures are.

> John Dryden, *Tyrannic Love,* act IV, sc. i. (1669)

* Love is a sweet torment.

> Thomas Draxe, *Bibliotheca.* (1616)

* Love is a smoke rais'd with the fume of sighs;

Being purged, a fire sparkling in lovers' eyes;

Being wex'd, a sea nourish'd with lovers' tears:

What is it else? a madness most discreet,

A choking gall and a preserving sweet.

> Shakespeare, *Romeo and Juliet,* act I, sc. i, 1. 196. (1595)

17. *L'amore è una pillola inzuccherata.*

(Love is a sugar-coated pill).

Love is sweet in the beginning, but sour in the ending.

> Thomas Draxe, *Bibliotheca.* (1616)

* O what a heaven is love! O what a hell!

> Thomas Dekker. *The Honest Whore*, pt. I, act I, sc. 1. 1604)

It [love] shall...

Find sweet beginning, but unsavoury end.

> Shakespeare, *Venus and Adonis,* 1. 1138. (1593)

* Love is a sour delight, a sugar'd grief,

A living death, an ever-dying life.

> Thomas Watson, *The Passionate Century of Love*, sonnet XVIII. (1582)

18. *L'amore raddolcisce il cuore. (Calabrese)*

(Love softens the heart).

Love makes all hearts gentle.

> George Herbert, *Jacula Prudentum.* (1640)

* Amore e cor gentil sono una cosa.

(Love and a gentle heart are one thing).

> Dante, *Vita Nova,* sonetto XX. (c. 1292)

19. *Chi ama, crede.*

(He who loves, believes).

Where love is there is faith.

> *The Oxford Dictionary of English Proverbs.* (1948)

* Whoso loves believes the impossible.

Elizabeth Barrett Browning, A*urora Leigh,* bk. V, 1.408. (1857)

* Love is a credulous thing.

Ovid, *Heroides:* Epistle vi, 1. 21. (c. 10 B.C.)

20. *Amor vuol fede, e fede vuol fermezza.*

Love asks faith, and faith firmness.

John Ray, *English Proverbs.* (1678) George Herbert, *Jacula Prudentum.* (1640)

21. *Chi ama assai, parla poco.*

(He who loves much, says little).

Whom we love best, to them we can say the least.

John Ray, *English Proverbs.* (1670)

* They love least that let men know their love.

Shakespeare, *The Two Gentlemen of Verona,* act I, sc. ii, 1. 32. (1594)

* True love lacks a tongue.

John Lyly, *Euphues and His England,* p. 392. (1580),Arber's reprint.

* Those that love most speak least.

George Pettie, *Petite Pallace,* p. 168. (1576)

* *Chi pò dir com'egli arde è 'n picciol foco.*

(He who can say how much he loves, loves but little).

Francesco Petrarca, *Il Canzoniere,* sonetto CXXXV. (c. 1350)

22. *Il cuore non sbaglia.*

(The heart makes no mistakes).

The heart sees farther than the head.

Mario Hazon, *Grande Dizionario Inglese-Italiano, Italiano-Inglese.* (1974)

* The head cannot impersonate the heart for long.

La Rochefoucauld, *Maxims:* maxim 108. (1665)

* Who can deceive a lover?

Virgil, *Aeneid,* bk. IV, 1. 296. (c. 19 B.C.)

* *Il cuore dell'uomo ... lo avverte spesso meglio di sette sentinelle in guardia su un'altura.*

Scritti apocrifi: Ecclesiastico, 37:14. Edizioni Paoline

A man's own mind has ... a way of telling him more

than seven watchmen posted high on a tower.

Apocrypha: Ecclesiasticus, 37:14. The New English Bible

23. *Della sua stessa colpa amor è scusa.*

(Love excuses its own fault).

Love sees no fault.

> Henry George Bohn, *Handbook of Proverbs.* (1855)

* Love to fault is always blind.

> William Blake, *Miscellaneous Poems and Fragments.* (1793 - 1818)
> Poem

24. *Contro amor... non è consiglio.*

(There is no advice against love).

The heart has arguments with which the understanding is unacquainted.

> Ralph Waldo Emerson, *The Conduct of Life: Worship.*(1860)

* Love is without reason.

> Thomas Draxe, *Bibliotheca.* (1616)

* Though Love use Reason for his physician,

He admits him not for his counsellor.

> Shakespeare, *The Merry Wives of Windsor*, act II, sc. i, 1.5. (1601)

* Find me a lover who can reason, and I shall give you his weight in gold.

> Plautus, *Curculio*, 1. 201. (c. 200 B.C.)

25. *Chi ha fatto il saggio del miele non può dimenticare il lecco.*

(He who has sampled honey cannot forget its taste).

There's nothing in this world so sweet as love.

> Henry Wadsworth Longfellow, *The Spanish Student*, act II, sc. v. (1843)

* Ah, what is love? It is a pretty thing,

As sweet unto a shepherd as a king.

> Robert Greene, *The Shepherd's Wife Song.* (c. 1592)

* *Che cosa è più dolce del miele?*

> *Antico Testamento: Giudici,* 14:18. Edizioni Paoline

What is sweeter than honey?

> *Old Testament: Judges,* 14:18. King James version

26. *Quel che nel cuor si porta, invan si fugge.*

(It is vain to flee from one's own heart).

A loyal heart never lies.

> A Scottish proverb

* Obey thy heart.

   Ralph Waldo Emerson, *Poems: Give All to Love,* stanza 1. (1847)

* A good heart cannot lie.

   George Herbert, *Jacula Prudentum.* (1640)

* *Ascolta ... il consiglio del tuo cuore, perché niente ti può essere piu fedele.*

   Scritti apocrifi: Ecclesiastico, 37:13. Edizioni Paoline.

Stick to the advice your heart gives you, no one can be truer to you than that.

   Apocrypha, Ecclesiasticus, 37:13. The Gerusalem Bible

27. *Di tutte le arti maestro è amore.*

   * *Amor è una cosa che aguzza ogni ingegno.*

(Love is the master of all the arts).

Love makes one inventive.

   Molière (Jean Baptiste Poquelin), *L'école des Maris,* act I, sc. iv, 1. 31. (1661)

* It has and shall be evermore

That Love is master where he will.

   John Gower, *Confessio Amantis,* bk. I, 1. 35. (c. 1388)

The god of love, a! benedicite,

How mighty and how great a lord is he!

   Geoffrey Chaucer, *The Canterbury Tales: The Knight's Tales*, 1. 927. (c. 1386)

* Love is the best teacher.

   Pliny, The Younger, *Letters,* bk. IV, letter 19. (c. A.D. 98)

28. *Dove la voglia è pronta, le gambe son leggiere.*

   * *Chi ha l'amor nel petto, ha gli sproni ai fianchi.*

Where the will is ready, the feet are light.

   John Ray, *English Proverbs.* (1670)

* He that has love in his breast, has spurs at his heels.

   John Ray. *English Proverbs.* (1670)

* He that has love in his breast. has spurs at his sides.

   George Herbert. *Jacula Prudentum.* (1640)

29. *A chi vuole, nulla è impossibile.*

   * *Nulla è difficile a chi vuole.*

Nothing is impossible to a willing mind.

> John Ray. *English Proverbs*. (1670)

* Non mancano pretesti quando si vuole.

(Where there is a will, one can find a way).

> Carlo Goldoni, *La Villeggiatura,* act I, sc. xii. (1762)

* Nothing is difficult to a well willed man.

> David Ferguson, *Scottish Proverbs*. (c. 1595)

* Nothing is impossible to a willing heart.

> John Heywood, *Proverbs,* pt. I, ch. 4. (1546)

30. *L'amore trova il luogo.*

* Quando l'amore vuole trova il luogo. (Calabrese)

Love will find its way.

> Lord Byron, *The Giaour,* 1. 1047. (1813)

* Love ... will find or force a passage.

> Thomas Fuller, *The Worthies of England,* bk. II, 1. 227. (1662)

* Love will find out the way.

> Thomas Bayly, *Love Will Find Out the Way.* Title of play. (c. 1650)

* Were beauty under twenty locks kept fast,

Yet love breaks through and picks them all at last.

> Shakespeare, *Venus and Adonis,* 1. 575. (1593)

31. Tutto vince amor.

* Amor vince ogni cosa.

> John Florio, *Firste Fruites.* (1578)

Love conquers all.

> Florio. *ibid.* Virgil, *Eclogues*: eclogue X. 1. 69. (c. 37 B.C.)

* Love will conquer at the last.

> Lord Tennyson. *Locksley Hall Sixty Years After,* 1. 280. (1886)

32. *Amor regge il suo regno senza spada.*

Love rules his kingdom without a sword.

> George Herbert. *Jacula Prudentum.* (1640)

* Love rules without a sword;

Love binds without a cord.

> An English jingle

33. *Amor regge senza legge.*

* Dove c'è amore non c'è legge. (Siciliano)

Love is lawless.

> John Clarke, *Paroemiologia.* (1639)

* Love is above King or Kaiser, lord or laws.

    Robert Greene, *Works,* vol. II, 1. 122. (1583)

* Love knows no laws.

    John Lyly, *Euphues: The Anatomy of Wit,* p. 84. (1579) Arber's reprint.

* Love is above lord or laws.

    George Pettie, *Petite Pallace,* p. 219. (1576)

* Love's law is out of rule.

John Gower, *Confessio Amantis,* bk. 1,1.13. (c. 1388)

    * Who can give law to lovers? Love is a greater law to itself.

    Boethius, *De Consolatione Philosophiae,* bk. III, meter 12, 1. 47. (c. A.D. 520)

* Love knows nothing of order.

    St. Jerome, *Letter to Chromatius.* (c. A.D. 374)

34. *Amor non mira lignaggio, né fede, né vassallaggio.*

(Love looks at neither lineage, nor faith, nor vassalage).

Love is a platform upon which all ranks meet.

    William Schwenck Gilbert, *H.M.S. Pinafore,* act II. (1878)

* Love rules the court, the camp, the grove

And men below, and saints above;

For love is heaven, and heaven is love.

    Sir Walter Scott, *The Lay of the Last Minstrel,* canto III, stanza 2. (1805)

* Love lives in cottages as well as in courts.

    John Ray, *English Proverbs.* (1670)

35. *Amor tutti eguaglia.*

    * Ogni disuguaglianza amore agguaglia.

Love makes all men equal.

    An English proverb

* Love levels all ranks.

    O. Henry (William Sydney Porter), *Best Seller.* (1909)

* Amor che a nullo amato amar perdona.

(Love, that excuses no one beloved from loving).

    Dante, *La Divina Commedia: Inferno,* canto V, 1. 103. (c. 1312)

* Love is the same in everyone.

Virgil, *Georgics,* bk. III, 1. 244. (c. 30 B.C.)

36. *Amore e signoria non voglion compagnia.*

Love and lordship like no fellowship.
> John Ray, *English Proverbs.* (1670)

* Love and lordship hate companions.
> Benjamin Franklin, *Poor Richard's Almanack.* (1737)

* Love and lordship never like fellowship.
> Nathan Baily, *Dictionary.* (1736)

* Love never desires a partner.
> Thomas Fuller, *Gnomologia.* (1732)

* Love and lordship like no partners.
> James Kelly, *Scottish Proverbs.* (1721)

* Né amore né signoria vuol compagnia.
> John Florio, *Firste Fruites.* (1578)

Neither love nor friendship will have company.
> Florio, *ibid.*

* Ful sooth is seyd, that love ne lordshipe
Wol noght ... have no felaweshipe.
> Geoffrey Chaucer, *The Canterbury Tales. The Knight's,* 1. 765.
> (c. 1386)

37. *Pensano gli innamorati che gli altri siano ciechi.*

(Lovers think that others are blind).

* Gli innamorati vedono solo se stessi in questo mondo
e dimenticano che il mondo li vede.

(Lovers see only themselves in this world
and forget that the world sees them).
> August von Platen, *Berengar.* From F. Palazzi e S. Spaventa Filippi, *Il Libro dei Mille Savi,* No. 7467. (1955)

38. *L'amore e la tosse presto si conosce.*

* Amor, tosse e fumo malamente si nascondono.

(Love and cough are quickly shown).

Love and a sneeze cannot be hid.
> An English proverb

* Love and a cold cannot be hid.
> Patricia Wentworth, *The Chinese Shawl,* p. 175. (1943)

* Love, cough, and smoke, can't well be hid.
  Benjamin Franklin, *Poor Richard's Almanack.* (1737)
* There is no disguise which can for long conceal love where -
  it exists or simulate it where it does not.
  La Rochefoucauld, *Maxims:* maxim 70. (1665)
* Love and a cough cannot be hid.
  George Herbert, *Jacula Prudentum.* (1640)
* Fire cannot be hidden in the flax without smoke nor
love in the breast without suspicion.
  John Lyly, *Euphues and His England,* p. 425. (1580) Arber's reprint.

39. *Sdegno d'amante poco dura. (Toscano)*

  (A lover's indignation does not last long).

  A lover's anger is short-lived.
  Henry George Bohn, *Handbook of Proverbs.*(1855)
* Love follows anger.
  Pierre Corneille, *Bodogune,* act III, sc. i. (1664)
* A lover's quarrel has but short-lived strength.
  Menander, *Fragments:* fragment 797. (c. 300 B.C.)

40. *Sdegno cresce amore.*

  (Disdain increases love).

  Lovers' quarrels ... add a sweetness to those domestic joys.
  Charles Dickens, *Nicholas Nickleby,* ch. 10. (1839)

  Love-quarrels oft in pleasing concord end.
  John Milton, *Samson Agonistes,* 1. 1008. (1671)
* The falling out of lovers is the renewing of love.
  Robert Burton, *The Anatomy of Melancholy,* pt. III, , sec. 21. member
  3, (1621)
* Mark how they fell out. and how they fell in.
  John Heywood, *Proverbs,* pt. II, ch. 1. (1546)
* After a quarrel reconciliation becomes more beautiful.
  Publilius Syrus, *Sententiae.* (c. 43 B.C.)
* The quarrels of lovers are renewals of love.
  Terence, *Andria (The Lady of Andros),* 1. 555. (c. 166 B.C.)
* [After a quarrel, lovers] are twice as fond
of one another as they were before.

Plautus, *Amphitryon,* 1. 943. (c. 200 B.C.)

41. *Amami poco, ma continua.*

Love me little, love me long.

> Charles Reade, *Love Me Little. Love Me Long.* Title of novel. (1859)
> James Kelly, *Scottish Proverbs.* 1721.
> Christopher Marlowe, *The Jew of Malta,* 1. 1948. (c. 1590)
> Anonymous, *Ballad: Love Me Little.* (c. 1570) John Heywood, *Proverbs,* pt. II, ch. 2. (1546)

* Pray love me little, so you love me long.

> Robert Herrick, Hesperides: *Love Me Little. Love Me Long.* (1648)

* Love moderately; long love doth so.

> Shakespeare, *Romeo and Juliet,* act II, sc. vi, 1. 14. (1595)

* Amami poco, e amami a lungo.

> John Florio, *Firste Fruites.* (1578)

Love me little, and love me long.

> Florio, *ibid.*

42. *Ben ama chi non oblia.*

(He loves well who does not forget).

Sound love is not soon forgotten.

> An English saying

* I will never desert Mr. Micawber.

> Charles Dickens, *David Copperfield,* ch. 12. (1849)

* Love without end, has no end.

> George Herbert, *Jacula Prudentum.* (1640)

* Love's fire heats water, water cools not love.

> Shakespeare, *Sonnets:* sonnet CLIV, (1609)

* Le grandi acque non saprebbero spegnere l'amore,
  né i fiumi sommergerlo.

> *Antico Testamento: Cantico dei Cantici,* 8:7. Edizioni Paoline

Many waters cannot quench love, neither can the floods drown it.

> *Old Testament: Song of Solomon,* 8:7. King James version.

43. *Amor vero non diventa mai canuto.*

True love never grows old.

> An English proverb

* Love, strong as Death.

> Alexander Pope, *Ode for Music on St. Cecilia's Day,* stanza 4, 1. 51. (1708)

* But true love is a durable fire,

In the mind ever burning,

Never sick, never old, never dead,

From itself never turning.

> Sir Walter Raleigh, *As You Came from the Holy Land,* stanza 1.
> (c. 1599)

* My love to thee is sound sans crack or flaw.

> Shakespeare, *Love's Labour's Lost,* act V, sc. ii, 1. 415. (1595)

* L'amore è forte come la morte.

> *Antico Testamento: Cantico dei Cantici,* 8:6. Diodati, tr.

Love is strong as death.

> *Old Testament: Song of Solomon,* 8:6. King James version.

44. *Il primo amore non si scorda mai.*

* Tre cose non si scordano mai: la patria, la mamma e il primo amore.

(One's first love can never be forgotten).

First love last love.

> An English proverb

* One always returns to one's first love.

> Charles GuillaumeÉtienne, *La Joconde,* act III, sc. i. (1814)

* I find as I grow older that I love those most whom I loved first.

> Thomas Jefferson, *Letter to Mrs. John Bolling.* (1787)

* Lo spirito mio ... d'antico amor sentì la gran potenza.

(My spirit ... felt the great power of its old love).

> Dante, *La Divina Commedia: Purgatorio*, canto XXX, 1. 39. (c. 1315)

45. *Nella guerra d'amore chi fugge è vincitore. (Siciliano)*

* Nella guerra d'amore vince chi fugge.

In love's wars, he who flees is conqueror.

> Thomas Fuller, *Gnomologia.* (1732)

* The only victory of love is flight.

> Attributed to Napoleon Bonaparte. (c. 1810)

*   Only they

Conquer Love that run away.

> Thomas Carew, *Poems: Conquest by Flight.* (c. 1640)

46. *Gli amori nuovi fanno dimenticare i vecchi.*

* L'ultima bocca bella ogni altra cancella. (Siciliano)

* Come chiodo scaccia chiodo, così amore scaccia amore.

(New loves make one forget the old).

One love drives out another.

    Henry George Bohn, *Handbook of Proverbs.* (1855)

* Love may be expelled by other love.

John Dryden, *All for Love,* act IV, sc. i. (1678)

* As one nail by strength drives out another,

So the remembrance of my former love

Is by a newer object quite forgotten.

    Shakespeare, *The Two gentlemen of Verona,* act II, sc. iv, 1. 192.
    (1594)

* One love expels another.

    John Lyly, *Euphues, The Anatomy of Wit,* p. 116. (1579) Arber's
    reprint

* New loves forget the old.

    Gabriel Meurier, *Tresor des Sentences.* (c. 1550)

* Il nuovo amor sempre caccia l'antico.

(New love always drives out the old)

    Giovanni Boccaccio, *Il Filostrato,* canto IV, stanza 49. (c. 1350)

* All love is conquered by a succeding new love.

    Ovid, *Remedia Amoris,* 1. 462. (c. 2 B.C.)

47. *Se ne vanno gli amori e restano i dolori.*

    (Loves go away but heart-aches stay).

Those who are faithless know the pleasures of love;

it is the faithful who know love's tragedies.

    Oscar Fingal Wilde, *The Picture of Dorian Gray,* ch. 1. (1891)

* The course of true love never did run smooth.

    Shakespeare, *A Midsummer-Night's Dream,* act I, sc. i, 1. 132. (1596)

* The joy of love is too short, and the sorrow thereof...

dureth over long.

    Sir Thomas Malory, *Le Morte d'Arthur,* bk. X, ch. 56. (c. 1470)
    Printed by William Caxton, the first English printer, in 1485.

* In love, pain and pleasure are always at war.

    Publilius Syrus, *Sententiae.* (c. 43 B.C.)

48. *Le rose cadono e le spine rimangono.*

    * Al fin ogni fiore perde l'odore.

(The roses perish, but the thorns remain).

* Anyone who has never really loved has never really lived.
    Agatha Christie, *Sad Cypress,* ch. 2. (1939)
* 'Tis better to have loved and lost than never to have lost at all.
    Samuel Butler, *The Way of All Flesh,* ch. 77. (1903)
* 'Tis better to have loved and lost
Than never to have loved at all.
    Lord Tennyson, In Memoriam, pt. XXVII, stanza 4. (1850)
* Eyery joy is gain,
And gain is gain, however small.
Robert Browning, *Paracelsus,* pt. IV. (1835)
* Let no one who loves be called altogether unhappy.
Even love unreturned has its rainbow.
    James Matthew Barrie, *The Little Minister,* ch. 24. (1821)
* Better to love amiss than nothing to have loved.
    George Crabbe, *Tales: The Struggles of Conscience,* 1. 46. (1812)
* Say what you will, 'tis better to be left,
than never to have been lov'd.
    William Congreve, *The Way of the World,* act II, sc. i. (1700)

49. *Lontano dagli occhi, lontano dal cuore.*

    * Assenza nemica d'amore, quanto lontan dall'occhio tanto dal cuore.
    (Far from the eyes, far from the heart)
Salt water and absence always wash away love.
        Horatio Nelson, *Letter.* (1805) From Robert Southey, *Life of Nelson,*
        ch. 2. (1813)
    * Long absent, soon forgotten.
        John Ray, *English Proverbs.* (1670)
    * Out of sight, out of mind.
        John Heywood, *Proverbs,* pt. I, ch. 3. (1546)
    * Seldom seen, soon forgotten.
        John Heywood, *Proverbs,* pt. I, ch. 11. (1546)

50. *La lontananza ogni gran piaga sana.*

    (Distance heals every wound).
Time is an herb that cures all diseases.
        Benjamin Franklin, *Poor Richard's Almanack.* (1738)
    * On the wings of Time grief flies away.

Jean de La Fontaine, *Fables,* bk. VI, fable 21. (1668)

* A little time, my lord, will kill that grief.
    Shakespeare, *The Two Gentlemen of Verona,* act III, sc. ii, l. 14. (1594)

51. *L'amor fa molto, il denaro fa tutto.*

    * L'amore non fa bollire la pentola.

    Love does much, money does everything.
    The Oxford Dictionary of English Proverbs. (1948)

    * Love does much, but money does more.
    Thomas Fuller, *Gnomologia.* (1732)

    * Money is the senew of love.
    Thomas Fuller, *Gnomologia.* (1732)

     * Of soup and love, the first is the best.
    Thomas Fuller, *Gnomologia.* (1732)

    * Love does much, but money does all.
    Randle Cotgrave, *French-English Dictionary* (1611)

52. *Senza Cerere e Bacco, è amor debole e fiacco.*

    (Without Ceres and Bacchus, love is very weak).

    Love in a hut, with water and a crust,

    Is - Love, forgive us! - cinders, ashes, dust.
    John Keats, *Poems*: *Lamia,* pt. II, l. 1. (1820)

    * Love's desires and pleasures cool

    Sans Ceres' wheat and Bacchus' wine.
    George Peele, *King Edward the First,* act II, l. 86. (1593)

    * Without Ceres and Bacchus, Venus becomes cold.
    Terence, *Eunuchus,* l. 732. (c. 161 B.C.)

53. *Quando la fame vien dentro la porta, l'amore se ne va dalla finestra.*

    When Poverty comes in at the door, Love creeps out at the window.
    Thomas Fuller, *Gnomologia.* (1732)

    * When poverty comes in at the door, love jumps out at the window.
    John Galt, *The Entail,* ch. 14. (1823)

    * Love is maintain'd by wealth; when all is spent,

    Adversity then breeds the discontent.
    Robert Herrick, *Adversity.* (1648)

    * When poverty comes in at doors, love leaps out at windows.

John Clarke, *Paroemiologia.* (1639)

* As poverty goes in at one door, love goes out at the other.

Richard Brathwait, *The English Gentlewoman,* p. 346. (1631)

* Love abideth not with want, for she is the companion of plenty.

Sir Walter Ralegh, *Instruction to His Son,* sec. II. (1616)

* In well-fed bodies love resides.

Euripides, *Fragments:* fragment 895. (c. 440 B.C.)

54. *Chi nasce bella non nasce povera.*

    * Chi nasce bella non è del tutto poverella.

    (She who is born beautiful is not born poor).

    A good face needs no band, and a pretty wench no land.

        Henry George Bohn, *Handbook of Proverbs.* (1855)

    * "What is your fortune, my pretty maid?

    My face is my fortune, sir, she said."

    An old nursery rhyme.

    * Maidens be they never so foolish, yet being fair,

    they are commonly fortunate.

        John Lyly, *Euphues and his England*, p. 279. (1580) Arber's reprint

55. *Bellezza è mezza ricchezza.*

    (Beauty is half of wealth).

    A good face is worth more than gold.

        William Scarborough, *Chinese Proverbs.* (1875)

    * A fair face is half a portion.

        John Ray, *English Proverbs.* (1670)

    * Gold can do much,

    But beauty more.

        Philip Massinger, *The Unnatural Combat*, act I, sc. i. (1639)

    * She that is fair has half her portion.

        Thomas Draxe, *Bibliotheca.* (1616)

56. *La bellezza è mezza dote.*

(Beauty is half a dowry)

    Beauty carries its dower in its face.

        An English proverb

    * A beautiful girl, though very poor,

    is nevertheless abundantly dowered.

        Apuleius, *Pro Se De Magia Liber*, sec. 92. (c. A.D. 165)

57. *Chi nasce bella nasce maritata.*

    She that is born handsome is born married.

        John Ray, *English Proverbs.* (1670)

    * She that is born a beauty, is half married.

Thomas Fuller, *Gnomologia*. (1732)

58. *Chi ha bella donna e castello in frontiera, non ha mai pace in lettiera.*

(He who has a beautiful wife and a frontier castle never sleeps well).

He that has a white horse and a fair wife, never wants troubles.

Thomas Fuller, *Gnomologia*. (1732)

* A fair wife and a frontier castle breed quarrels.

George Herbert, *Jacula Prudentum*. (1640)

* He that a white horse and a fair wife keeps,

For fear, for care, for jealousy scarce sleeps.

John Florio, *Second Frutes*. (1591)

59. *Chi è bella ti fa far sentinella.*

* Chi ha la moglie bella sa che non è tutta sua. (Meridionale)

(She who is beautiful makes you vigilant)

You cannot pluck roses without fear of thorns,

Nor enjoy a fair wife without danger of horns.

Benjamin Franklin, *Poor Richard's Almanack*. (1734)

* Beauty may have fair leaves, yet bitter fruit.

Thomas Fuller, *Gnomologia*. (1732)

* Who has a fair wife needs more than two eyes.

John Ray, *English Proverbs*. (1670)

* Beauty, a deceitful bait with a deadly hook,

and a sweet poison in a painted pot.

John Lyly, *The Anatomy of Wit*, p. 77. (1579)Arbert's reprint

* She who is born beautiful is born with sorrow for many a man.

Confucius, *The Analects*. (c. 500 B.C.) From Tehyi Hsieh, *Confucius Said It First*.

60. *Bella donna e veste tagliuzzata sempre s'imbatte in qualche uncino.*

A fair woman and a slashed gown find always some nail in the way.

John Ray, *English Proverbs*. (1670)

* Too dear I prized a fair enchanting face:

Beauty unchaste is beauty in disgrace.

Alexander Pope, *Translation of Odyssey*, bk. VIII, 1. 359. (1725)

61. *Bellezza e follia sovente in compagnia.*

* Beltà e follia vanno spesso in compagnia. (Toscano)

(Beauty and folly go often together).

Beauty and folly are old companions.

Benjamin Franklin, *Poor Richard's Almanack*. (1734)

* Beauty and folly are sisters.

A German proverb

62. *La bellezza è effimera.*

(Beauty is ephemeral).

Beauty's out skin deep.

Thomas Fuller, *Gnomologia*. (1732) John Davies of Hereford, *A Select Second Husband for Sir Thomas Overburie's Wife*, stanza 13, (1616)

* Beauty that's only skin deep

Must fade like the gowans of May.

Allan Ramsay, *The Gentle Shepherd*, act IV, sc. ii, (1725)

* Beauty is but skin deep, ugly lies the bone;

Beauty dies and fades away, but ugly holds its own.

An old English jingle.

* Beauty of face is a frail ornament,

A thing belonging only to the skin.

Molière (Jean Baptiste Poquelin), *Les Femmes Savantes*, act III, sc. iv, 1. 19. (1672)

* All the beauty of the world, 'tis but skin deep.

Ralph Venning, *Orthodox Paradoxes: The Triumph of Assurance*, p. 41. (1650 edition)

* Beauty is a fleeting thing.

Seneca, *Hippolytus*. 1. 773. (c. A.D. 60)

63. *La bellezza è come un fiore che nasce e presto muore.*

(Beauty is like a flower that blooms and soon dies).

Beauty is a flower ... a breath.

A Latin saying

* I heard the old, old men say.

"All that's beautiful drifts away

Like the waters."

William Butler Yeats, *The Old Men Admiring Themselves in the Water*. (1904)

* Beauty's of a fading nature -

Has a season, and is gone!

Robert Burns, *Will Ye Go and Marry Katie?* (c. 1793)

* What's beauty? - Call ye that your own,

A flow'r that fades as soon as blown!

Benjamin Franklin, *Poor Richard's Almanack*. (1740)

* Beauty's a blossom.

  Thomas Fuller, *Gnomologia*. (1732)

* Beauty is but a blossom.

  Thomas Draxe, *Bibliotheca*. (1616)

* Beauty is but a flower,

Which.wrinkles will devour.

  Thomas Nashe, *Summer's Last Will and Testament*, 1. 600. (1600)

* Beauty's a flower.

  Shakespeare, *Twelfth Night*, act I, sc. v, 1. 57. (1599)

64. *La bellezza non fa bollire la pentola.*

  (Beauty does not make the pot boil)

  Beauty is potent, but money is omnipotent.

  Henry George Bohn, *Handbook of Proverbs*. (1855)

* Beauty is potent, but money is more potent.

  Thomas Fuller, *Gnomologia*. (1732)

* Beauty will buy no beef.

  Thomas Fuller, *Gnomologia*. (1732)

* Beauty without riches goes begging.

  John Lyly, *Euphues and His England*, p. 295. (1580) Arber's reprint

65. *L'occhio è lo specchio dell'anima.*

  The eye is the mirror of the soul.

  An English proverb

* The eye is the pearl of the face.

  Thomas Fuller, *Gnomologia*. (1732)

* In the forehead of the eye, the lecture of the mind does lie.

  John Ray, *English Proverbs*. (1670)

* L'occhio è lume del corpo.

  Nuovo Testamento: Matteo, 6:22. Edizioni Paoline

  The light of the body is the eye.

  New Testament: Matthew, 6:22. King James version

66. *Non è bello il corpo se l'anima non è bella.*

  (The body is not beautiful if the soul is not beautiful).

  The body is the workhouse of the soul.

  Thomas Fuller, *Gnomologia*. (1732)

  The body is the socket of the soul.

John Ray, *English Proverbs*. (1670)

For the soul the body form does take:

For soul is form, and does the body make.

    Edmund Spenser, *An Hymne in Honour of Beautie*, 1. 132. (1596)

* Outward beauty is not enough.

    Petronius, *Fragments:* fragment 16. (c. A.D. 60)

67. Bontà passa beltà.

Bellezza senza bontà è come vino svanito.

* Onestà e gentilezza sopravanza ogni bellezza.

(Goodness surpasses beauty).

What a strange illusion it is to suppose that beauty is goodness.

    Leo Nikolaevich Tolstoy, *The Kreutzer Sonata*, ch. 5. (1890)

* Beauty without grace is a hook without bait.

    Ralph Waldo Emerson, *The Conduct of Life: Beauty*. (1860)

* A fair woman without virtue is like palled wine.

    Henry George Bohn, *Handbook of Proverbs*. (1855)

* Goodness is the only investment that never fails.

    Henry David Thoreau, *Walden: Higher Laws*. (1854)

* Beauty, madame, pleases only the eyes; sweetness charms the soul.

    Voltaire (François Marie Arouet), *Nanine*, act I, sc. i. (1749)

* Nothing so popular as goodness.

    Benjamin Franklin, *Poor Richard's Almanack*. (1737)

* Beauty in women is like the flowers in the spring;

but virtue is like the stars of heaven.

    Thomas Fuller, *Gnomologia*. (1732)

* Bounty before beauty is always to be preferred.

    George Pettie, *Petite Pallace*, p. 175. (1576)

* It is not beauty that bewitches bridegrooms but nobleness.

    Euripides, *Andromache*, 1. 208. (c. 430 B.C.)

68. Non è bello quel che è bello, ma è bello quel che piace.

Fair is not fair, but that which pleases.

    George Herbert, *Jacula Prudentum*. (1640)

* Beauty is altogether in the eye of the beholder.

    Lew Wallace, *The Prince of India*, bk. III, ch. 6. (1893)

* Beauty is in the eye of the beholder.

    Margaret Wolfe Hungerford, *Molly Bawn*, ch. 12.(1878)

* One man's beauty [is] another's ugliness.

    Ralph Waldo Emerson, *Essays:* First Series, Circles. (1841)

* Beauty is where it is perceived.

    Henry David Thoreau, *Autumn*, December 16,1840

* There is no worth nor beauty but in the mind's idea.

    Thomas Love Peacock, *Nightmare Abbey*, ch. 11. (1818)

* Beauty in things exists merely in the mind which contemplates them.

    David Hume, *Essays Moral and Political: Of Tragedy.* (1742)

69. A lume spento è pari ogni bellezza.

    * Al buio la villana è bella quanto la dama.

(When the light is out, every beauty is equal:).

Under the blanket, the black one is as good as the white.

    Thomas Fuller, *Gnomologia.* (1732)

* Joan is as good as my lady in the dark.

    Duchess of Newcastle (Margaret Cavendish), *Sociable Letters*, 11, 4. (1664)

* Joan as my Lady is as good i' th' dark.

    Robert Herrick, *Hesperides*: No Difference i' th' dark, (1648)

* All shapes, all colours, are alike in night.

    Sir Thomas Overbury, *A Wife*, stanza 17. (1614)

* When all candles are out ... all things are then of one colour.

    John Heywood, *Proverbs*, pt. I, ch. 5. (1546)

* All women are the same in the dark.

    Plutarch, *Moralia*: Conjugal Precepts. (c. A. D. 95)

* In the dark all blemishes are hidden ...

that hour makes any woman fair.

    Ovid, *Ars Amatoria*, bk. I, 1. 249. (c. 1 B.C.)

70. Al buio tutte le gatte sono bigie.

    * A lumi spenti tutti i gatti sono grigi.

All cats are grey in the dark.

    Thomas Lodge, *A Marguerite of America*, 1. 56. (1597)

* At night all cats are grey.

    Miguel de Cervantes, *Don Quixote de la Mancha*, pt. II, ch. 33. (1615)

* When all candles are out, all cats are grey.

    John Heywood, *Proverbs*, pt. I, ch. 5. (1546)

71. Tira più un pelo di donna che cento paia di buoi.

* Natura tira più che cento cavalli.

One hair of a woman can draw more than a hundred pair of oxen.

> James Howell, *Letters*, bk. II, No.4. (1637)

* Fair tresses man's imperial race ensare,

And beauty draws us with a single hair.

> Alexander Pope, *The Rape of the Lock*, canto II, 1. 27. (1712)

* She ... can draw you to her with a single hair.

> John Dryden, *Persius*, satire V, 1. 246. (1693)

* Nature draws more than ten teams.

> George Herbert, *Jacula Prudentum*. (1640)

* No cord nor cable can so forcibly draw, or hold so fast,

as love can do with a twined thread.

> Robert Burton, *The Anatomy of Melancholy*, pt. III, sec. 2, member 1, subsec. 2. (1621)

* Ten teams of oxen draw much less

Than does one hair of Helen's tress.

> John Florio, *Second Frutes*. (1591)

72. Donna buona vale una corona. (Bresciano)

(A good woman is worth a crown)

The proverb says: a man's own hearth and a good woman
are more than gold and pearls.

> Johann Wolfgang yon *Goethe*, Faust. pt. I, sc. xii. (1806)

* Said Solomon the wise, A good wife's a goodly prize.

> John Ray, *English Proverbs*. (1678)

* A good woman is worth, if she were sold,

The fairest crown that's made of purest gold.

> John Wodroephe. *The Spared Houres of a Souldier*, p.484. (1623)

* Una donna buona è una vera fortuna.

> *Scritti apocrifi: Ecclesiastico*. 26:3. Edizioni Paoline

A good wife is a good portion.

> *Apocrypha: Ecclesiasticus*, 26:3. American Bible Society

* Una donna saggia e buona ... val più dell'oro.

Scritti apocrifi: Ecclesiastico, 7:19. Edizioni Paoline

A wise and good wife ... is worth more than gold.

Apocrypha, Ecclesiasticus, 7:19. Revised Standard Version - Catholic Edition

* Donna di valore, chi la troverà?

più delle perle è infatti prezioso il suo pregio.

Antico Testamento: Proverbi, 31:10. Garzanti

Who can find a virtuous woman? for her price is far above rubies.

Old Testament: Proverbs, 31:10. King James Version

* La donna virtuosa è la gloria del marito.

Antico Testamento: Proverbi, 12:4. Edizioni Paoline

A virtuous woman is a crown to her husband.

Old Testament: Proverbs, 12:4. King James Version

73. *All'onor chi manca d'un momento non lo ripara in anni cento.*

* Ragazza che dura non perde ventura.

A hundred years cannot repair a moment's loss of honor.

Henry George Bohn, *Handbook of Proverbs*. (1855)

* A woman with a past has no future.

Attributed to Oscar Wilde. (c. 1892)

* Honor is venerable to us because it is no ephemeris.

It is always ancient virtue.

Ralph Waldo Emerson. *Essays: Self-Reliance*. (1841)

* Honor is like an island, rugged and without a beach;

once we have left it, we can never return.

Nicolas Boileau-Despreaux, *Satires*: satire, X, 1. 167. (c. 1675)

* If I lose mine honour, I lose myself.

Shakespeare, *Antony and Cleopatra*, act III, sc. iv, 1. 22. (1606)

* Mine honour is my life; both grew in one;

Take honour from me. and my life is done.

Shakespeare, *King Richard II*, act I, sc. i, 1. 182. (1595)

* Honor, like life, when once lost, never returns.

Publilius Syrus, *Sententiae*. (c. 43 B.C.)

* Non macchiare la tua reputazione.

Scritti apocrifi: Ecclesiastico,33:23. Edizioni Paoline

Bring no stain upon your honor.

Apocrypha, Ecclesiasticus, 33:23. Revised Standard Version - Catholic Edition

74. *Di novello tutto è bello.*

    * A giovane cuore tutto è gioco.

    Novelty always appears handsome.

        Henry George Bohn, *Handbook of Proverbs*. (1855)

    * Nothing more playful than a young cat.

        Thomas Fuller, *Gnomologia*. (1732)

    * Everything new is fine.

        George Herbert, *Jacula Prudentum*. (1640)

    * I will hold your minds with sweet novelty.

        Ovid, *Metamorphoses*, bk. IV, 1. 284. (c. A.D. 7)

75. *L'uomo è fuoco e la donna è stoppa.*

    (Man is fire and woman is tow).

    * When the man's fire, and the wife's tow,

    In comes the devil and blows it in a lowe (blaze).

        A Scottish jingle.

    * The tow and tinder of which men and women

    are proverbially composed,

    only wait a chance spark, a rising breeze, to become a bonefire.

        George John Whyte-Melville, *Uncle John*, ch. 6. (1874)

    * When the husband is fire, and the wife tow

    the devil easily sets all in a flame.

        Thomas Fuller, *Gnomologia*. (1732)

76. *Figlie e vetri son sempre in pericolo.*

    A woman and a glass are ever in danger.

        George Herbert, *Jacula Prudentum*. (1640)

    * Glasses and lasses are brittle ware.

        John Ray, *English Proverbs*. (1670)

    * The first handsome woman ... was made of Venice glass.

        James Howell, *Waters*, June 1, 1621.

    * Woman is made of glass.

        Miguel de Cervantes, *Don Quixote de la Mancha*, pt. I, ch. 33. (1605)

77. *Chi vuol la figlia carezzi la madre.*

    He that would the daughter win,

Must with the mother first begin.

> John Ray, *English Proverbs.* (1670)

* Woo first the mother if you'd win the daughter.

> Henry Austin Dobson, *The Story of Rosina.* (1877)

* I make presents to the mother, but think of the daughter.

> Johann Wolfgang von Goethe, *Sprüche in Reimen*, pt. III. (c. 1825)

78. *Amante non sia chi coraggio non ha.*

(Let him not be a lover who does not have courage).

*Shyness is a great sin against love.

> Anatole France (Jacques Anatole François Thibault), *La Rotisserie de la Reine Pedauque.* (1893)

* Faint heart never won fair lady.

> William Schwenck Gilbert, *Iolanthe*, act II. (1882) John Ray, *English Proverbs*, (1670)

* Love requires boldness, and scorns bashfulness.

> Thomas Fuller, *Gnomologia.* (1732)

* Faint heart never wins castle nor lady.

> John Lyly, *Euphues and His England*, p. 364. (1580) Arber's reprint

79. *Le donne resistono per essere conquistate.*

(Women resist in order to be conquered).

* Every woman may be won.

> Sir Walter Scott, *Quentin Durward*, ch. 19. (1823)

* Every woman is infallibly to be gained by every sort of flattery.

> Philip Dormer Stanhope, Earl of Chesterfield, *Letters*, March 16, 1752.

* She's beautiful and therefore to be woo'd:

She is a woman, therefore to be won.

> Shakespeare, *King Henry VI*, Part I, act V, sc. iii, 1. 78. (1591)

* There is no woman but she will yield in time.

> John Lyly, Euphues: *The Anatomy of Wit*, p. 64. (1579) Arber's reprint

* Women were in their creation ordained to be wooed,and to be won.

> John Ford, *A Line of Life*, p. 59. (1620)

* All women can be caught.

> Ovid, *Ars Amatoria*, bk. I. 1. 269. (c. 1 B.C.)

80. *Donna che prende tosto s'arrende.*

* Donna che dona di rado è buona; donna che piglia è nell'altrui artiglia.

(A woman who accepts gifts soon yields).

* The woman who accepts gifts sells herself.

> A French proverb

* What female heart can gold despise?

What cat's averse to fish?

> Thomas Gray, *On the Death of a Favourite Cat Drowned in a Tub of Gold Fishes*, stanza 4. (1747)

* A maid that takes yields.

> John Ray, *English Proverbs.* (1670)

81. *Donna di finestra, uva di strada.*

* Ragazza corteggiata, di rado maritata.

* Castello che dà orecchia si vuol rendere.

A woman that loves to be at the window

is like a bunch of grapes on the highway.

> William Carew Hazlitt, *English Proverbs.* (1869)

* Maidens and castles must yield in the end.

> Johann Wolfgang von Goethe, *Faust*, pt. I, sc. ii. (1806)

* The female and fortress which begins to parley is half-gain'd.

> James Howell, *Parly of Beasts*, p. 66. (1660)

* Castles that come to parley, and women that delight

in courting, are willing to yield.

> John Lyly, *Euphues and His England*, p. 334. (1580) Arber's reprint

82. *Trotto d'asino, fuoco di paglia, e amor di donna poco durano.*

> John Florio, *Firste Fruites.* (1578)

The trot of an ass, the fire of straw, and the love of a woman last little.

> Florio, *ibid*

* Love lodged in a woman's breast

Is but a guest.

> Sir Henry Wotton, *A Woman's Heart.* (c. 1639)

* Ophelia: 'Tis brief, my lord.

Hamlet: As woman's love.

> Shakespeare. *Hamlet.* act III. sc. ii. 1. 165. (1600)

83. *Donna è luna, oggi serena e domani bruna.*

(A woman is like the moon, today clear and tomorrow cloudy).

* "Yes." I answered you last night;

"No." this morning sir, I say:

Colors seen by candlelight

Will not look the same by day.

    Elizabeth Barrett Browning. *The Lady's "Yes"*. stanza 1. (1844)

* Woman's faith, and woman's trust -

Write the characters in dust.

    Sir Walter Scott. *The Betrothed*. ch. 20. (1825)

* A woman's mind is like the wind in a winter's night.

    James Kelly, *Scottish Proverbs*. (1721)

* A woman's mind and winter wind change often.

    John Ray, *English Proverbs*. (1670)

* Vuole e disvuole, è folle uom che sen fida ...

(She will and she won't, fool is the man who trusts in her ...).

    Torquato Tasso, *La Gerusalemme Liberata*, canto XIX, stanza 84.
    (1581)

* Ne l'onde solca, e ne l'arena semina,

E 'l vago vento spera in rete accogliere

Chi sue speranze fonda in cor di femina.

(He plows the waves, and sows the sand,

And seeks to gather the wind in a net

Who sets his hopes in the heart of woman).

    Jacopo Sannazzaro, *Arcadia*, ecloga octava. (1504)

84. *Tempo, vento, signor, donna, fortuna*

    Voltano e tornan come fa la luna.

    (Times, wind, lord, woman and fortune

    are as changeable as the moon).

    * Woman is various and most mutable.

       Lord Tennyson, *Queen Mary*, act III, sc. vi, 1. 77. (1875)

    * Women, wind and fortune are ever changing.

       Henry George Bohn, *Handbook of Proverbs*. (1855)

    * La donna è mobile

    Qual piuma al vento.

    (Woman is fickle as a feather in the wind).

       Francesco M. Piave, Libretto of Verdi's *Rigoletto*, Duke's song. (1851)

* Woman often changes ... as a feather in the wind.
>> Victor Hugo, *Le Roi s'amuse*, act IV, sc. ii. (1832)

* Volubil sempre come foglia al vento.

(Always fickle as a feather in the wind).
>> Giovanni Boccaccio, *Il Filostrato*, canto VIII, stanza 30. (c. 1350)

* Woman is always fickle and unstable.
>> Virgil, *Aeneid*, bk. IV, 1. 569. (c. 19 B.C.)

85. *Donna iraconda, mare senza sponda.*

(An irate woman is like a sea without a shore).

* A slighted woman knows no bounds.
>> Sir John Vanbrugh, *The Mistake*, pt. II, act II, sc. i. (1706)

* He shall find no Fiend in Hell

can match the fury of a disappointed woman.
>> Colley Cibber, *Love's Last Shift*, act IV, sc. i. (1696)

* Non c'e ira peggiore di quella della donna.
>> *Scritti apocrifi: Ecclesiastico*, 25:14. Edizioni Paoline

There is no anger above the anger of a woman.
>> *Apocrypha: Ecclesiasticus*, 25:14. Douay Version

* There is no wild beast more savage than a woman in her anger;

she is wilder than a leopard, fiercer than fire.
>> Aristophanes, *Lysistrata*, 1. 1014. (c. 412 B.C.)

* Strange that God has given to men

Salves for the venon of all creeping snakes.

But nobody has ever yet devised a cure

For the venon of woman, worse than fire or viper;

So terrible a mischief are we to men.
>> Euripides, *Andromache*, 1. 269. (c. 430 B.C.)

86. *Savie all'impensata, alla pensata pazze son le donne.*

Women are wise impromptu, fools on reflection.
>> Henry George Bohn, *Handbook of Proverbs*. (1855)

* A woman who thinks is as loathsome as a man who wears make-up.
>> Gotthold Ephraim Lessing, *Emilia Gaiotti*, act IV, sc. iii. (1772)

* The woman that deliberates is lost.
>> Joseph Addison, *Cato*, act IV, sc. i, 1. 29. (1713)

87. *Dove sono donne ed oche non vi son parole poche.*

* Tre donne e un'oca fanno un mercato.

Where women are and geese, there wants no gaggling.

> Thomas Fuller, *Gnomologia*. (1732)

Three women and a goose make a market.

> John Ray, *English Proverbs*. (1678)

* When man and woman die, as poets sung,

His heart's the last part moves, - her last, the tongue.

> Benjamin Franklin, *Poor Richard's Almanack*. (1739)

* Her tongue runs like the clapper of a mill.

> Jonathan Swift, *Polite Conversation*, Dialogue I. (1738)

* Where there are women and geese there wants no noise.

> John Ray, *English Proverbs*. (1678)

* A woman's tongue wags like a lamb's tail.

> John Ray, *English Proverbs*. (1670)

* When a man dies, the last thing that moves is his heart;

in a woman her tongue.

> George Chapman, *The Widdowes Teares*, act IV, sc. ii. (1612)

88. *Femmine e galline per troppo andar si perdono.*

Women and hens, through too much gadding, are lost.

> John Ray, *English Proverbs*. (1670)

* A woman and a hen will always be gadding.

> An English proverb

* A woman and a hen are soon lost by gadding.

> Miguel de Cervantes, *Don Quixote de la Mancha*, pt. II, ch. 49. (1615)

89. *Donne, preti, e polli non son mai satolli.*

Women, priests, and poultry have never enough.

> Thomas Fuller, *Gnomologia*. (1732)

* Women, priests, and poulty never have enough.

John Ray, *English Proverbs*. (1670)

* O woman, woman, woman, woman, woman!

Tortuous as hell, insatiate as the grave!

> Nathaniel Field, *A Woman is a Weather-Cock*, act III. (1612)

90. *Se la donna fosse piccola come è buona,*

la minima foglia le farebbe una veste e una corona.

If a woman were as little as she is good,

a pease-cod would make her a gown and a hood.

    John Ray, *English Proverbs*. (1670)

* If women were as little as they are good,

A peas-cod would make them a gown and a hood.

    John Florio, *Second Frutes*. (1591)

91. *La donna per piccola che sia, non la vince il diavolo in furberia.*

    * Le donne sanno un punta piu del diavolo.

(Though a woman is small, the devil cannot surpass her in cunning).

* Women are the devil's net.

    An English proverb

* The devil has become a woman.

    Victor Hugo, *Ruy Blas*, act II, sc. v. (1838)

* O woman, woman! whether lean or fat,

In face an angel, but in soul a cat.

    Peter Pindar (John Wolcot), *The Lousiad*, canto II. (1800)

The devil dances in a woman's placket.

    James Howell, *English Proverbs*. (1659)

* A wicked woman and an evil

is three halfpence worse than the devil.

    John Clarke, *Paroemiologia*. (1639)

* Trust a woman? I'll trust the devil first.

    John Fletcher, *The Changes*, act II, sc. i. (1620)

* A woman can do more than the devil.

    William Bercher, *The Nobility of Women*, p. 140. (1559)

92. *Lagrime di donna, fontana di malizia. (Toscano)*

    * Niente più tosto si secca che lacrime.

(The tears of a woman are a fountain of malice).

* Women have tears of dissimulation.

    Thomas Fuller, *Gnomologia*. (1732)

* Nothing dries sooner than a woman's tears.

    Thomas Fuller, *Gnomologia*. (1732)

* There are three things that are not to be credited,

a woman when she weeps, a merchant when he swears,

nor a drunkard when he prays.

    Barnaby Rich, *My Lady's Looking Glass*, ch. 34. (1616)

* There's nothing sooner dries than women's tears.

    John Webster, *The White Devil*, act V, sc. iii. (1612)

* Women's weapons, water-drops.

    Shakespeare, *King Lear*, act II, sc. iv, 1. 280. (1605)

* A woman's tear is the sauce of malice.

    Publilius Syrus, *Sententiae*. (c. 43 B.C.)

* When a woman weeps she is constructing a snare with her tears.

    Marcus Porcius Cato, the Elder, *Disticha*, bk. III, distich 20. (c. 175 B.C.)

93. Le donne piangono con la stessa facilita con cui i cani pisciano. (Milanese)

    (Women cry with the same ease as dogs urinate).

* Women laugh when they can, and weep when they will.

    George Herbert, *Jacula Prudentum*. (1640)

* As much pity to be taken of a woman weeping,

as of a goose going barefooted.

    Robert Burton, *The Anatomy of Melancholy*, pt. III, sec. 2, member 3, subsec. 4. (1621)

* Trust not a woman when she cries,

For she'll pump water from her eyes.

    Thomas Dekker, *The Honest Whore*, pt. I, act V. (1604)

* At every hour, the dog makes water and the woman weeps.

    Gabriel Meurier, *Trésor des Sentences*. (c. 1550)

* Do not be moved by women's tears;

they have taught their eyes to weep.

    Ovid, *Remedia Amoris*, 1. 689. (c. 2 B.C.)

* Women love tears.

    Sophocles, *Ajax*, 1. 580. (c. 409 B.C.)

94. Donna si lagna, donna si duole,

donna s'ammala quando lei vuole.

A woman's in pain, a woman's in woe;

a woman is ill when she likes to be so.

    Henry George Bohn, *Handbook of Proverbs*. (1855)

* Women naturally deceive, weep and spin.

    The Oxford Dictionary of English Proverbs. (1948)

* It's a custom of the sex to cry when they have sorrow,
to weep when they have joy, and to shed tears whenever
they find themselves without either.

> O. Henry (William Sydney Porter), *A Tempered Wind.* (1908)

* Deceite, weping, spinning god hath yive

To wommen kindely, why1 they may live.

> Geoffrey Chaucer, *The Canterbury Tales: The Wife of Bath's Prologue*, 1.401. (c. 1388)

* And where does not art penetrate?

They learn to weep becomingly,

and can wail when and how they choose.

> Ovid, *Ars Amatoria*, bk. III, 1. 291. (c. 1 B.C.)

95. *La donna è come la castagna,*

Bella di fuori e dentro è la magagna.

(A woman is like a chestnut: beautiful outside, but rotten inside).

* They are saints abroad, but ask their maids what they are at home.

> Charles Haddon Spurgeon, *John Ploughman's Pictures*, ch. 16. (1880)

* Wives ... are angels in the streets, saints in the

church, and devils at home.

> Charles Haddon Spurgeon, *John Ploughman's Talk*, ch. 13. (1869)

* Dissimulation is innate in woman.

> Arthur Schopenhauer, *Studies in Pessimisms: On Women.* (c. 1818)

* Women are in churches, saints; abroad, angels; at home, devils.

> George Wilkins, *The Miseries of Inforst Mariage*, act I. (1607)

* You are pictures out of doors,

Bells in your parlours, wild-cats in your kitchens.

> Shakespeare, *Othello*, act II, sc. i, 1. 110. (1605)

A woman is a fury and an hurtful spirit in the house,

an angel in the church ...

> William Bercher, *The Nobility of Women,* p. 127. (1559)

Women are saints in church, angels in the street and devils at home.

> Gabriel Meurier, *Trésor des Sentences.* (c. 1550)

96. *Donne, asini, e noci voglion le mani atroci.*

*Buon cavallo e mal cavallo vuole sproni;

buona femmina e mala femmina vuol bastoni.

Women, asses, and walnut-trees require a hard hand).

*A woman, a whelp, and a walnut-tree,

the more you bash 'em the better they be.

> An English proverb

*When you go to women, take your whip with you.

> George Bernard Shaw, *Pygmalion*, act v. (1912)

*'Tis natural for asses, women, and walnut-trees

to mend upon beating.

> Sir Roger *L'Estrange*, Translation of Aesop. p. 284. (1692)

* A spaniel, a woman and a walnut tree,

The more they're beaten the better still they be.

> John Ray, *English Proverbs*. (1670)

97. *Un uomo di paglia vale una donna d'oro.*

A man of straw is worth a woman of gold.

> John Ray, *English Proverbs*. (1670) James Howell, *Familiar Letters*, bk. II, No.4. (1647)

* They say a man of straw is worth a woman of gold.

> Charles Haddon Spurgeon, *John Ploughman's Talk*, ch. 17. (1869)

* Idolatrize not so the sex, but hold

A man of straw more than a wife of gold.

> Samuel Daniel, *Hymen's Triumph*. (1615)

* A man of straw is more worth than a woman of gold.

> John Florio, *Second Fruites*. (1591)

98. *Gli uomini hanno gli anni che sentono, e le donne quelli che mostrano.*

(Men are as old as they feel; women as old as they look).

* They used to say that a woman is as old as she looks

and a man is as old as he feels.

> Gelett Burgess, *Look Eleven Years Younger*, p. 231. (1937)

* A man is as old as he's feeling; a woman as old as she looks.

> Mortimer Collins, *How Old Are You?* (1855)

99. *Chi disse donna disse danno.*

(He who said woman, said ruin).

* From Adam's wife, that proved a curse.

> Robert Bridges, *Triolet*. (c. 1900)

* Fire, water, woman, are man's ruin,

Says wise Professor Vander Bruin.

Matthew Prior, *Fire, Water. Woman.* (1709)

* O why did God ... create at last

This noveltie on Earth, this fair defect

Of Nature, and not ... find some other way to generate Mankind?

John Milton, *Paradise Lost*, bk. X, 1. 888. (1667)

* I see women the way to wrack and ruin.

George Pettie. *Petite Pallace.* p. 269. (1576)

* A woman as who said wo to the man.

John Heywood. *Proverbs*, pt. II. ch. 7. (1546)

* Woman, mischief to man.

Euripides. *Hippolytus*, 1. 616. (c. 428.:B.C.)

100. *Bacco, tabacco. e Venere riducono l'uomo in cenere.*

* Fuggi donne, vino, dado; se no, il tuo fato è spacciato.

(Bacchus, tobacco, and Venus reduce man to ashes).

* Play, women, and wine are enough to make a prince a pauper.

Charles Haddon Spurgeon, *John Ploughman's Pictures.* ch. 11. (1880)

* Women and wine, game and deceit,

Make the wealth small, and the wants great.

James Kelly, *Scottish Proverbs.* (1721)

* Play, women, and wine undo men laughing.

James Howell, *English Proverbs.* (1659)

* Gaming, women, and wine, while they laugh they make men pine.

George Herbert, *Jacula Prudentum.* (1640)

* Wine, women, and dice. will bring a man to lice.

John Florio, *Second Frutes.* (1591)

* Il vino e le donne pervertono anche i sapienti.

*Scritti apocrifi: Ecclesiastico,*19:2. Edizioni Paoline

Wine and Women will make men of understanding to fall away.

Apocrypha: Ecclesiasticus, 19:2. American Bible Society

101. *Chi non ama il vino, la donna, e il canto, un pazzo egli sarà*

e mai un santo.

(He who does not love wine. women and song,

will be a fool but never a saint).

* ... Doctor Martin Luther sang:

"Who loves not wine, woman, and song,
He is a fool his whole life long."

William Makepeace Thackeray. *Adventures of Philip*, ch. 7. (1862)

* Let us have wine and women, mirth and laughter.

Lord Byron, *Don Juan*, canto II, stanza 178. (1819)

* Who does not love wine, women, and song

Remains a fool his whole life long.

Attributed to both Martin Luther and Johann Heinrich Voss.

* Fill ev'ry glass, for wine inspires us ...

With courage, love and joy.

Women and wine should life employ.

John Gay, *The Beggar's Opera*, act II, sc. i, air 19. (1728)

102. Innanzi il maritare, abbi l'abitare.

Before you marry, make sure of a house wherein to tarry.

Thomas Fuller, *Gnomologia.* (1732)

* Ne'er take a wife till thou hast a house ... to put her in.

Benjamin Franklin, *Poor Richard's Almanack.* (1743)

* Never look for a wife till you have a house ... to put her in.

James Kelly, *Scottish Proverbs.* (1721)

* Be sure before you marry, of a house wherein to tarry.

John Ray, *English Proverbs.* (1670)

* Choose a house made and a wife to make.

George Herbert, *Jacula Prudentum.* (1640)

* Buy a house made and a wife unman'd.

Randle Cotgrave, *French-English Dictionary.* (1611)

103. Chi fabbrica la casa in piazza, o che è troppo alta o troppo bassa.

* Chi fabbrica vicino alla strada ha molti sindicatori. (Veneziano)

He that builds a house by the highway side,

it is either too high or too low.

John Ray, *English Proverbs.* (1670)

* Build a cottage by the roadside

and you will not get it finished in three years.

William Scarborough, *Chinese Proverbs.* (1875)

* A house built by the way-side, is either too high, or too low.

Thomas Fuller, *Gnomologia.* (1732)

104. Casa nuova, chi non ve ne porta, non ve ne trova.

* Chi edifica, la borsa purifica. (Toscano)

(You find nothing in a new house except what you bring).

* Building is sweet impoverishing.

Thomas Fielding, *Proverbs of All Nations.* (1824)

* He that builds before he counts the cost, acts foolishly;

and he that counts before he builds, finds that he did not count wisely.

Benjamin Franklin, *Poor Richard's Almanack.* (1753)

* Patch, and long sit; build, and soon flit.

John Ray, *English Proverbs*. (1670)

* The charges of building ... are unknown.
  George Herbert, *Jacula Prudentum*. (1640)

* Building is a great impoverishing.
  George Herbert, *Jacula Prudentum*. (1640)

* The building of houses ... are unlimited wasters
of a man's substance.
  Randle Cotgrave, *French-English Dictionary*. (1611)

* Building is a thief.
  John Manningham, *Diary*, p. 9. (1602)

105. *Ad ogni uccello suo nido e bello.*

* Ogni uccello fa festa al suo nido.
Every bird likes its own nest best.
  Thomas Fuller, *Gnomologia*. (1732)

* The bird loves her nest.
  George Herbert, *Jacula Prudentum*. (1640)

106. *Più vale il fumo di casa mia che il fuoco dell'altrui.*

* Più vale il fumo di casa mia che l'arrosto dell'altrui.

* E'meglio pane e cipolla a casa sua che gallina in casa d'altri.
The smoke of a man's own house is better than the fire of another's.
  John Ray, *English Proverbs*. (1670)

* The little I have is free, and I can call it my own!
"Home' s home, be it never so homely!
  John Arbuthnot, *Law is a Bottomless Pit*, pt. III, ch. 4. (1712)

* Dry bread at home is better than roast meat abroad.
  George Herbert, *Jacula Prudentum*. (1640)

* It is better to be at home in the cave of an hermit
than abroad in the court of an emperor.
  John Lyly, *Euphues and His England*, p. 243. (1580) Arber's reprint

107. *La lepre sta volentieri dov'è nata.*

* Si vive bene all'ombra del campanile.
(The hare remains willingly where it was born).

* The hare always returns to her form.
  The Oxford Dictionary of English Proverbs. (1948)

* Home is where one starts from.

Thomas Stearns Eliot, *Four Quartets: East Coker*, pt. V. (1940)

* You can't appreciate home till you've left it.

O. Henry (William Sydney Porter), *Roads of Destiny: The Fourth in Salvador*. (1909)

* I have no thoughts of stirring from the house I was born;

like the hare, I shall be worried in the seat I started from.

Sir Walter Scott, *The Heart of Mid-Lothian*, ch.. 34. (1818)

* No place is more pleasant than one's own home.

Cicero, *Ad Familiares*, bk. IV. epistle 8. (c. 46 B.C.)

* He who is truly happy should stay at home.

Aeschylus, *Fragments*: fragment 177. (c. 485 B.C.)

108. Legami mani e piei e gettami tra i miei. (Toscano)

(Tie my hands and feet but keep me among my own people).

* We shall breathe the air again

Of the free land in our own beloved home.

George Frederick Root, *Tramp! Tramp! Tramp!* (1862)

* The voice I hear this passing night was ...

Perhaps the self-same song that found a path

Through the sad heart of Ruth, when, sick for home,

She stood in tears amid the alien corn.

John Keats, *Poems*: Ode to a Nightingale, stanza 7. (1820)

* My ain fireside, my ain fireside,

O there's naught to compare wi' ane's ain fireside.

Elizabeth Hamilton, *My Ain Fireside*. (c. 1800)

* Such is the patriot's boast, where'er we roam,

His first, best country ever is, at home.

Oliver Goldsmith, *The Traveller*, 1. 73. (1764)

* Ay, now am I in Arden: the more fool I;

when I was at home I was in a better place.

Shakespeare, *As You Like It*, act II, sc. iv, 1. 15. (1600)

* Always own is own, at the reckoning's end.

John Heywood, *Proverbs*, pt. II, ch. 4. (1546)

* It is better to be at home in fear than in your Athens without fear.

Cicero, *Ad Atticum*, bk. XVI, epistle 6. (c. 44 B.C.)

109. *Casa propria non c'è oro che la paghi.*

(No amount of gold can pay for one's own home).

* One's own hearth is worth gold.

An English proverb

110. *Ognuno è padrone a casa sua.*

Ognuno è re in casa propria.

Everyman is master in his own home.

Mario Hazon. *Grande Dizionario Inglese-Italiano, Italiano-Inglese* (1974)

* Every man is master at home.

An Icelandic proverb

* The house is a castle which the King cannot enter.

Ralph Waldo Emerson, *English Traits; Wealth.* (1856)

* A man's house is his castle.

John Ray, *English Proverbs.* (1610)

* For a man's house is his castle, et domus sua cuique

tutissimum refugium (and his home is the safest refuge).

Sir Edward Coke, *Institutes of the Laws*: Third Institute, ch. 73. (1644)

* I, in my own house, am an emperor.

Philip Massinger, *The Roman Actor*, act I. sc. ii. (1626)

* Everyone is a king in his own house.

Randle Cotgrave, *French-English Dictionary.* (1611)

* Every groom is a king at home.

John Davies of Hereford, *The Scourge of Folly.* p. 42. (1611)

111. *Casa mia, mamma mia. (Toscano)*

* Casa mia, casa mia,

Per piccina che tu sia.

Tu mi sembri una badia. (Toscano)

(My house is as dear to me as my mother).

* Home is home, be it never so homely.

An English proverb. Charles Dickens, *Dombey and Son*, ch. 35. (1848)

* Home is where the heart is.

Elbert Hubbard, *A Thousand and One Epigrams.* (1911) Often attributed to Pliny.

* If a home is happy, it cannot fit too close.

    O. Henry (William Sydney Porter), *A Service of Love* (1906)

* He never cares to wander from his own fireside,

He never cares to wander or to roam.

With his baby on his knee,

He's as happy as can be,

* For there's no place like home, sweet home.

    Felix McGlennon, *He Never Cares to Wander from His Own Fireside.* (1892)

* Let your boat of life be light,

packed with only what you need - a homely home.

    Jerome Klapka Jerome, *Three Men in a Boat*, ch. 3. (1889)

* Stay, stay at home, my heart, and rest;

Home-keeping hearts are happiest.

    Henry Wadsworth Longfellow, *Song*, stanza 1. (1877)

* Where we love is home,

Home that our feet may leave, but not our hearts.

    Oliver Wendell Holmes, *Homesick in Heaven*, stanza 5. (1872)

* This is the true nature of home - it is the place of

peace; the shelter, not only from all injury, but from

all terror, doubt and division.

    John Ruskin, *Sesame and Lilies: of Queen's Gardens.* (1865)

* East or West. home is best.

    Henry George Bohn. *Handbook of Proverbs.* (1855)

* Mid pleasures and palaces though we may roam,

Be it ever so humble, there's no place like home.

Home, home, sweet home!

    John Howard Payne. *Home, Sweet Home*. From the opera *Clari, The Maid of Milan*, act I. (1823)

* I still shall say - that home is home.

    William Combe. *Dr. Syntax !n Search of the Picturesque*, canto XXVI. (1812)

* His home, the spot of earth supremely blest,

A dearer, sweeter spot than all the rest.

    James Montgomery. *The West Indies*, pt. III. 1. 67. (1809)

* Home is a homely word.

> James Kelly, *Scottish Proverbs*. (1721)

* Home is home though it be never so homely.

> John Ray, *English Proverbs*. (1670)

* My house. my house, though thou art small,
thou art to me the Escurial.

> George Herbert, *Jacula Prudentum*. (1640)

* Seek home for rest for home is best.

> Thomas Tusser. *Five Hundred Points of Good Husbandry: Instructions to Housewifery*. (1573)

* Home is homely, though it be poor in sight.

> John Heywood. *Proverbs*, pt. I, ch. 4. (1546)

* Home is dearest.

> Cicero, *Ad Atticum*, bk. XV. epistle 16. (c. 44 B.C.)

112. *Dalla casa si conosce il padrone.*

* Quale l'uccello, tale il nido.

(The owner is known by his house).

* Grace thy house, and not let that grace thee.

> Benjamin Franklin. *Poor Richard's Almanack*. (1739)

* The house shows the owner.

> George Herbert, *Jacula Prudentum*. (1640)

* The house discovers the owner.

> Randle Cotgrave, *French-English Dictionary*. (1611)

* Such bird, such nest.

> Randle Cotgrave, *French-English Dictionary*. (1611)

* The owner should bring honor to the house,
not the house to the owner.

> Cicero, *De Officiis*, bk. II, ch. 39, sec. 139. (c. 45 B.C.)

113. *Dal servo si giudica il padrone.*

(One judges the master from his servant).

* Servants will not be diligent, where the master's negligent.

> Thomas Fuller, *Gnomologia*. (1732)

* Trimm tramm, like master like man.

> James Howell, *English Proverbs*. (1659)

* A sleepy master makes his servant a lout.

George Herbert, *Jacula Prudentum*. (1640)

* My name is Trimtram, forsooth; look, what my master does,
I used to do the like.

Thomas Middleton, *A Fair Quarrel*, act II, sc. ii. (1617)

* Tal padrone, tal servitore.

John Florio, *Firste Fruites*. (1578)

Like master, like man.

Florio, *ibid.*

* Such master, such man.

Thomas Tusser, *Five Hundred Points of Good Husbandry: April's Abstract*. (1573)

* The servant is like the master.

Petronius, *Satyricon*, sec. 58. (c. A.D. 60)

114. Vicinanza senza siepe porta inimicizia in casa.

* Per amicizia conservare, muri bisogna piantare.

(Neighbors without a fence won't be friends for long).

* A hedge between keeps friendship green.

An English proverb

* Good fences make good neighbors.

Robert Frost, *Mending Wall*. (1914)

* A wall between preserves love.

Samuel Palmer, *Moral Essays on Proverbs*, p. 168. (1710)

* Love your neighbor, yet pull not down your hedge.

George Herbert, *Jacula Prudentum*. (1640)

115. Buon vicino, buon mattino.

* Chi ha il huon vicino, ha il huon mattino.

A good neighbor, a good morrow.

John Ray, *English Proverbs*. (1670)

* All is well with him who is beloved of his neighbors.

George Herbert, *Jacula Prudentum*. (1640)

* You have a good neighbor then,
and by consequence a good morrow.

John Florio, *Second Fruites*. (1591)

* A bad neighbor is a misfortune as a good one is a blessing.

Hesiod, *Works and Days*, 1. 346. (c. 750 B.C.)

116. Chi ha il cattivo vicino, ha il mal mattino.

　* Dio ti salvi da cattivo vicino e da un principiante di violino.

　(He who has a bad neighbor, has a bad morning).

　* The most pious man cannot live in peace

　if it does not please his wicked neighbor.

　　　Johann Christoph Friedrich von Schiller, *Wilhelm Tell*, act IV, sc. iii,
　　　1. 124. (1804)

　* No man can live longer in peace than his neighbor pleases.

　　　James Kelly, *Scottish Proverbs*. (1721)

　* Here is a talk of the Turk and the Pope,

　but my next neighbor does me more harm than either of them both.

　　　George Herbert, *Jacula Prudentum*. (1640)

　* You must ask your neighbor if you shall live in peace.

　　　John Clarke, *Paroemiologia*. (1639)

　* Our bad neighbour makes us early stirrers.

　　　Shakespeare, *King Henry V*, act IV, sc. i, 1. 6. (1599)

117. Buon avvocato, cattivo vicino.

　A good lawyer, a bad neighbor.

　　　Benjamin Franklin, *Poor Richard's Almanack*. (1737)

　* A good lawyer, an evil neighbor.

　　　Randle Cotgrave, *French-English Dictionary*. (1611)

118. Non contrastare con l'uomo potente e sta discosto dall'acqua corrente.

　* Né mulo, né mulino, né fiume, né forno, né signore per vicino.

　(Don't oppose a powerful man

　and stay away from swift-running waters).

　* A great man and a great river are often ill neighbors.

　　　Thomas Fuller, *Gnomologia*. (1732)

　* A great lord is a bad neighbor.

　　　John Ray, *English Proverbs*. (1670)

119. Meglio un prossimo vicino che un lontano cugino.

　(It is better to have a neighbor who lives near

　than a cousin who lives far).

　* Lord, make us learn to live together.

　Words written on the cornerstone of a Catholic

　　　Church at Auschwitz, Poland. (1979)

* Practice tolerance and live together in peace
with one another as good neighbors.

> *Charter of the United Nations.* preamble. (June.1945)

* In the field of world policy I would dedicate this
nation to the policy of the good neighbor.

> Franklin Delano Roosevelt. *First Inaugural Address*, (March 4,1933)

* We can live without our friends, but not without our neighbors.

> James Kelly, *Scottish Proverb.* (1721)

* Dio ci insegna ad amar il nostro prossimo come noi medesimi.

> John Florio. *Firste Fruites.* (1578)

God teaches us to love our neighbors as ourselves.

> Florio, *ibid.*

* I ask from you nought but that you love your neighbor.

> Mohammed. *The Koran,* ch. 42. (c. A.D. 622)

* E' meglio un amico vicino, che un fratello lontano.

Antico Testamento: Proverbi, 27:10. Edizioni Paoline

Better is a neighbour that is near than a brother far off.

Old Testament: Proverbs, 27:10. King James Version

† Ama il prossimo tuo come te stesso.

> *Antico Testamento: Levitico,* 19:18. Diodati, tr.

Love thy neighbour as thyself.

> *Old Testaments Leviticus,* 19:18. King James Version

120. Accasa il figlio quando vuoi. e la figlia quando puoi.

> Marry your son when you will; your daughter when you can.
>> George Herbert. *Jacula Prudentum*. (1651)

> * It is a woman's business to get married as soon as possible,
>> and a man's to keep unmarried as long as he can.
>> George Bernard Shaw, *Man and Superman*. act II. (1903)

> * I have always thought that every woman should marry. and no man.
>> Benjamin Disraeli. *Lothair,* ch. 30. (1870)

121. Non è bene che l'uomo sia solo.

>> *Antico Testamento, Genesi*. 2:18. Diodati. tr.

> It is not good that the man should be alone.
>> *Old Testament, Genesis*. 2:18. King James Version

> * It is not good for man to be alone.
>> Elizabeth Barrett Browning. *Aurora Leigh*. bk. V, 1. 1082. (1857)

> * Man was not made to live alone.
>> Francis Edward Smedley, *Frank Fairlegh*, ch. 51. (1850)

> * Marriage may often be a stormy lake, but celibacy
> is almost always a muddy horsepond.
>> Thomas Love Peacock, *Melincourt*, ch. 7. (1817)

> * Marriage has many pains, but celibacy has no pleasures.
> Samuel Johnson, *Rasselas*, ch. 26. (1759)

> * A man without a wife is but half a man.
>> Benjamin Franklin. *Poor Richard's Almanack*. (1755)

> * He that has not got a wife, is not yet a compleat man.
>> Benjamin Franklin, *Poor Richard's Almanack*. (1744)

> * The first bond of society is marriage.
>> Cicero, *De Officiis*. bk. I, ch. 17, sec. 54. *(c.* 45 B.C.)

122. Né donna, né tela, a lume di candela.

> Neither women nor linen by candle-light.
>> John Ray, *English Proverbs*. (1678)

> * Keep your eyes wide open before marriage.
>> Benjamin Franklin, *Poor Richard's Almanack*. (1738)

* Fine linen, girls, and gold so bright

Choose not to take by candle-light.

  Benjamin Franklin, *Poor Richard's Almanack.* (1737)

* Choose neither women nor linen by candle.

  John Davies of Hereford, *The Scourge of Folly, Proverbs.* (c. 1611)

* Né femina, né tela non piglia alla candela.

  John Florio, *Firste Fruites.* (1578)

Neither a woman, nor linen, choose by a candle.

  Florio, *ibid*

123. *Moglie e buoi dei paesi tuoi.*

  * La moglie e il ronzino piglia dal vicino.

  (Choose your wife and oxen from your own home town).

  * It is better to marry over the mixen than over the moor.

    Mario Hazon, *Grande Dizionario Inglese-Italiano Italiano-Inglese.* (1974)

  * Better wed over the mixon than over the moor.

    Sir Walter Scott, *The Heart of Mid-Lothian*, ch. 31. (1818)

  He that goes far to marry will either deceive or be deceived.

    Benjamin Franklin, *Poor Richard's Almanack.* (1735)

  * He that goes a great way for a wire, is either cheated

  or means to cheat.

    Thomas Fuller, *Gnomologia.* (1732)

  * A wife is not to be chosen by the eye only.

    Thomas Fuller, *Gnomologia.* (1732)

  * Choose a wife rather by your ear than your eye.

    John Ray, *English Proverbs.* (1670)

  * Who goes to Westminster for a wife, to Paul's [church] for a man,

   and to Smithfield for a horse, may meet with a whore,

  a knave and a jade.

    James Howell, *English Proverbs.* (1659)

  * In choosing a wife, and buying a sword,

  we ought not to trust another.

    George Herbert, *Jacula Prudentum.* (1640)

  * Marry a woman who lives near you.

    Hesiod, *Works and Days*, 1. 700. (c. 750 B.C.)

124. Qual figlia vuoi, tal moglie piglia.

    * Di buona terra to' la vigna, di buona madre to' la figlia.

As you would have a daughter so choose a wife.

Henry George Bohn, *Handbook of Proverbs.* (1855)

    * Take a vine of a good soil, and the daughter of a good mother.
      John Ray, *English Proverbs.* (1670)

*Choose a good mother's daughter, though her father were the devil.
      A Gaelic proverb

    * Choose a wife as you wish your children to be.
      A Gaelic proverb

    * All women become like their mothers. That is their tragedy.
No man does. That's his.
      Oscar Fingal Wilde, *The Importance of Being Earnest*, act 1. (1895)

    * She has a mark after her mother.
      John Ray, *English Proverbs.* (1678)

    * When the mare has a bald face, the filly will have a blaze.
      John Ray, *English Proverbs.* (1670)

    * If the dam trot, the foal will not amble.
      Robert Burton, *The Anatomy of Melancholy*, pt. III, sec. 3, member 4, subsec. 2. (1621)

    * If the mother trot how should the daughter amble?
      Barnaby Rich, *The Honesty of This Age*, ch. 32. (1614)

    * The mother's side being surer than the father's.
      Thomas Middleton, *Michaelmas Term*, act I, sc. i. (1607)

    * Quale la madre, tale la figlia.
      Antico Testamento: Ezechiele, 16:44. Edizioni Paoline

As is the mother, so is her daughter.
      Old Testament: Ezekiel, 16:44. King James Version

125. Tal padre, tal figlio.

    * Quale il padre, tale il figlio.

Like father, like son.
      Henry George Bohn, *Handbook of Proverbs.* (1855)

    * As the old cock crows, so the young one chirrups.
      An English proverb

    * Good fruit never came from a bad tree.

An English proverb
* There was never a good knife made of bad steel.
>   Benjamin Franklin, *Poor Richard's Almanack*. (1755)
* The fork is commonly the rake's heir.
>   Thomas Fuller, *Gnomologia*. (1732)
* The child has a red tongue, like its father.
>   John Ray, *English Proverbs*. (1670)
* Such a father, such a son.
>   John Ray, *English Proverbs*. (1670)
* The son of the female is the shadow of the male.
>   Shakespeare. *King Henry IV*. Part II, act III, sc. ii, 1. 141. (1598)
* L'albero buono non puo far frutti cattivi.
>   *Nuovo Testamento: Matteo*, 7:18. Diodati, tr.

A good tree cannot bring forth evil fruit.
>   *New Testament: Matthew*. 7:18. King James Version

126. *Il figlio al padre s'assomiglia. alla madre la figlia.*

Like father, like son; like mother, like daughter.
>   Thomas Draxe, *Bibliotheca*. (1616)
* An apple never falls far from the tree.
>   An English proverb
* How can the foal amble. when the horse and mare trot?
>   Thomas Fuller, *Gnomologia*. (1732)
* Trot mother, trot father, how can the foal amble?
>   David Ferguson. *Scottish Proverbs*. (c. 1595)
* But where the bull and cow are both milk-white,

They never do beget a coal-black calf.
>   Shakespeare, *Titus Andronicus*, act V, sc. i, 1. 31. (1593)
* The litter is like to the sire and the dame.

How can the foal amble, if the horse and mare trot?
>   John Heywood, *Proverbs*, pt. I, ch. 11. (1546)
* From good parents comes a good son.
>   Aristotle, *Politics*, bk. I, ch. 2. (c. 330 B.C.)

127. *Chi si marita fa bene, e chi no fa meglio.*

* Lauda la moglie e tienti donzello.
* Assai vince chi non gioca.

He who marries does well, but he who marries not, better.

John Ray, *English Proverbs*. (1670)

* Advice to persons about to marry. - "Don't."

Punch, vol. VIII, p. 1. (1845)

* He may well win the race that runs by himself.

Benjamin Franklin, *Poor Richard's Almanack*. (1747)

* Every man plays the fool once in his life, but to
marry is playing the fool all one's life long.

William Congreve, *The Old Bachelor*, act III, sc. x. (1693)

* Honest men marry soon, wise men not at all.

John Ray, *English Proverbs*. (1670)

* Commend a wedded life, but keep thyself a bachelor.

James Howell, *English Proverbs*. (1659)

* A bachelor was saying, Next to no wife, a good wife is best.
Nay, said a gentlewoman, next to a good wife, no wife is the best.

Thomas Fuller, *The Holy and Profane State*, bk. III, ch.22. (1642)

* Advice none to marry or go to war.

George Herbert, *Jacula Prudentum*. (1640)

* He was reputed one of the wise men that made answer to the
question when a man should marry: "A young man not yet,
an elder man not at all."

Francis Bacon, *Essays: Of Marriage and Single Life*. (1597)

* I advise you, "Do not marry."

Menander, *The Flute Girl*, fragment 65. (c. 300 B.C.)

* For a young man not yet, for an old man never at all.

Attributed both to Diogenes (c. 350 B.C.) and Thales (c. 600 B.C.)

128. *Il matrimonio è un male necessario.*

(Marriage is a necessary evil).

* Wives and wind are necessary evils.

James Kelly, *Scottish Proverbs*. (1721)

* Marriage is an evil that most men welcome.

Motto of *The Spectator*, December 29, 1711.

* Women are necessary evils.

John Clarke, *Paroemiologia*. (1639)

* One was never married, and that's his hell; another is,

and that's his plague.

> Robert Burton, *The Anatomy of Melancholy*, pt. I, sec. 2, member 4, subsec. 7. (1621)

* O curse of marriage! ... Yet ...

'Tis destiny unshunnable, like death.

> Shakespeare, *Othello*, act III, sc. iii, 1. 275. (1605)

* Women ... are indeed necessary, but evils.

> John Florio, *Second Frutes*. (1591)

* Marriage, if one will face the truth, is an evil,

but a necessary evil.

> Menander, *Fragments*: fragment 651. (c. 300 B.C.)

129. *Meglio celibe che mal sposato.*

(It is better to be single than unhappily married).

* Men marry because they are tired; women because they are curious

Both are disappointed.

> Oscar Fingal Wilde, *A Woman of No Importance*, act III. (1893)

* Better be half hanged than ill-wed.

> John Ray, *English Proverbs*. (1670)

* An ill marriage is a spring of ill fortune.

> Thomas Draxe, *Bibliotheca*. (1616)

* He is so averse to marrying again that he declares a bachelor's couch

is the most comfortable in the world.

> Cicero, *Ad Atticum*, bk. XIV, epistle 13. (c. 44 B.C.)

130. *Chi si marita in fretta, stenta adagio.*

* Chi erra in fretta, a bell'agio si pente.

Marry in haste and repent at leisure.

> John Ray, *English Proverbs*. (1670)

* She had married in haste, and repented, not at leisure,

but with equal rapidity.

> James Payn, *Thicker than Water*, ch. 31. (1883)

* Grief often treads upon the heels of pleasure,

Marry'd in haste, we oft repent at leisure.

> Benjamin Franklin, *Poor Richard's Almanack*. (1734)

* Marriage leaps up upon the saddle, and soon after

repentance upon the crupper.

Thomas Fuller, *Gnomologia*. (1732)

* Marry'd in haste, we may repent at leisure.

William Congreve, *The Old Bachelor*, act V, sc. viii. (1693)

* In hasty recklessness men often marry,

And afterwards repent it all their lives.

Molière (Jean Baptiste Poquelin), *Les Femmes Savantes*, act V, sc. iv, 1. 89. (1672)

* Hasty marriage seldom proveth well.

Shakespeare, *King Henry VI*, Part III, act IV, sc. i, 1. 18. (1591)

* Hasty love is soon hot and cold.

John Heywood, *Proverbs*, pt. I, ch. 2. (1546)

* When men will needs marry,

I see now, how wisdom and haste may vary.

John Heywood, *Proverbs*, pt. I, ch. 13. (1546)

131. La maggior sventura o ventura dell'uomo è la moglie.

A man's best fortune, or his worst, is a wife.

James Howell, *English Proverbs*. (1659)

* The sum of all that makes a just man happy

Consists in the well choosing of his wife.

Philip Massinger, *A New Way to Pay Old Debts*, act IV, sc. i. (1632)

* In the election of a wife,

As in a project of war, to err but once

Is to be undone for ever.

Thomas Middleton, *Any Thing for a Quiet Life*, act I, sc. i. (1626)

* The greatest care ought to be in the choice of a wife,

and the only danger therein is beauty.

Sir Walter Raleigh, *Instruction to His Son*, sec. II. (1616)

* Woman to man is either a god or a wolf.

John Webster, *The White Devil*, act IV. (1612)

* The best or worst thing to man, for this life

Is good or ill choosing his good or ill wife.

John Heywood, *Proverbs*, pt. I, ch. 2. (1546)

* There is no such thing as picking out the best woman;

one is worse than another.

Plautus, *Aulularia*, 1. 139. (c. 210 B.C.)

* Woman brings to man his greatest blessing and his greatest plague.

    Euripides, *Alcmaeon*, fragment. (c. 430 B.C.)

* There is no worse evil than a bad woman;

and nothing ... better than a good one.

    Euripides, *Melanippe Desmotis*, fragment. (c. 430 B.C.)

* A man gets nothing better than a good woman

and nothing worse than a bad one.

    Hesiod, *Works and Days*, 1. 702. (c. 750 B.C.)

132. I matrimoni sono, non come si fanno, ma come riescono.

(Marriages are, not as they are made, but as they turn out to be).

* Well-married, a man is winged — ill-matched, he is shackled.

    Henry Ward Beecher, *Proverbs from Plymout Pulpit*. (1887)

* Marriage is a lottery.

    Samuel Smiles, *Thrift*, p. 252. (1875)

* Think how like a lottery... weddings are.

    Ben Jonson, *A Tale of a Tub*, act I, sc. i. (1633)

* Marriage ... may make you or mar you.

    James Howell, *Letters*, February 5,1625.

* Marriage and hanging go by destiny.

    Francis Beaumont and John Fletcher, *A Wife for a Month,* act II, sc. i.
    (1624) Robert Burton, The *Anatomy of Melancholy*, pt. III, sec. 2,
    member 5, subsec. 5. (1621)

* Wedding and hanging goes by destiny.

    Thomas Dekker, *The Shoemaker's Holiday*, act IV, sc. iii. (1599)

* Hanging and wiving goes by destiny.

    Shakespeare, *The Merchant of Venice*, act II, sc. ix, 1., 82. (1597)

* Marriage is a lottery in which men stake their liberty

and women their happiness.

    Attributed to Madame de Rieux. (c. 1580)

* Wedding is destiny, and hanging likewise.

    John Heywood, *Proverbs*, pt. I, ch. 3. (1546)

133. Nozze e magistrato dal cielo è destinato.

  * *Matrimoni e vescovati son dal cielo destinati.*

(Weddings and magistracy are arranged by heaven).

* They say, marriages are made in heaven; but I doubt,

when she was married, she had no friend there.

> Jonathan Swift, *Polite Conversation*, Dialogue I.(c. 1738)

* If marriages are made in heaven, some had few friends there.

> James Kelly, *Scottish Proverbs*. (1721)

* All marriages are made in heaven.

> George Farquhar, *Love and a Bottle*, act V, sc. i. (1699)

* Matches are made in heaven.

> Robert Burton, *The Anatomy of Melancholy*, pt. III, sec. 2, member 5, subsec. 5. (1621)

* Your marriage comes by destiny.

> Shakespeare, *All's Well that Ends Well*, act I, sc. iii, 1. 66. (1602)

* Marriages are made in heaven.

> John Lyly, *Mother Bombie*, act IV, sc. i. (1590)

* Marriages are guided by destiny.

> George Pettie, *Petite Pallace*, p. 94. (1576)

134. Uomo ammogliato, uccello in gabbia.

(A married man is like a bird in a cage).

* Is not marriage an open question, when it is alleged,

from the beginning of the world, that such as are in the institution

wish to get out, and such as are out wish to get in?

> Ralph Waldo Emerson, *Representative Men: Montaigne; or, The Skeptic*. (1850)

* Wedlock and a padlock mean the same.

> Lord Byron, *Don Juan*, canto V, stanza 158. (1821)

* Marriage is a fetter, is a snare.

> Edward Young, *Love of Fames Satire* VI, 1. 65. (1728)

* Wedlock is a padlock.

> John Ray, *English Proverbs*. (1670)

* Wedlock and ill wintering tame both man and beast.

> John Ray, *English Proverbs*. (1670)

* Marriage is a noose.

> Miguel de Cervantes, *Don Quixote de la Mancha*, pt. II, bk. III, ch. 19. (1615) Motteux, tr.

135. Come uno piglia moglie entra nel pensatoio. (Toscano)

* Chi ha moglie allato, sta sempre travagliato.

(As soon as one gets married, he puts on his thinking-cap).

* Marriage is ... a field of battle, and not a bed of roses.

    Robert Louis Stevenson, *Virginibus Puerisque*, I, ch. 1. (1881)

* He that takes a wife takes care.

    Benjamin Franklin, *Poor Richard's Almanack*. (1736)

* Oh. how many torments lie in the small circle of a wedding ring.

    Colley Cibber. *The Double Gallant*, act I, sc. ii. (1707)

* He that has a wife, has strife.

    John Ray. *English Proverbs*. (1670)

* There is no other purgatory but a woman.

    Francis Beaumont and John Fletcher, *The Scornful Lady*, act III. (1610)

* Who will trouble himself all days of his life, let him marry a woman.

    John Florio, *Firste Fruites*. (1578)

* We wedded men live in sorwe and care.

    Geoffrey Chaucer, *The Canterbury Tales*: The Merchant's Prologue, 1. 16. (c. 1387)

136. *Il prim'anno che l'uomo piglia moglie, o s'ammala o s'indebita.*

    * *Uomo coniugato, uomo inguaiato. (Napoletano)* ·

(The first year a man gets married, either he gets sick or he runs into debt).

* Needles and pins, needles and pins,

When a man marries his trouble begins.

    James Orchard Halliwell, *The Nursery Rhymes of England*, p. 122. (1845)

* A married man turns his staff into a stake.

    George Herbert, *Jacula Prudentum*. (1640)

* Since the very first day, a married man grows seven years older.

    Francis Bacon, *Letter to Lord Burghley*. 1606)

* A young man married is a man that's marr'd.

    Shakespeare, *All's Well that Ends Well*, act II, sc. iii, 1. 315. (1602)

* The wife is the shipwreck of the man, the tempest of the house.

    John Florio, *Firste Fruites*. (1578)

* Marrying marring.

    John Heywood, *Proverbs*. pt. II, ch. 7. (1546)

* One woman is a host of ills for any man.

Propertius, *Elegies*, bk. II, elegy 25, 1. 48.(c. 24 B.C.)

137. Al mulino e alla sposa sempre manca qualche cosa.

Mills and wives ever want.

George Herbert, *Jacula Prudentum*. (1640)

* A ship, a mill, and a woman are always repairing.

Thomas Fuller, *Gnomologia*. (1732)

* It's nothing so intricate and difficult to rig a ship,

as a woman, and the more either is fraught, the apter to leak.

Sir Thomas Overbury. *Newes from Any Whence: Newes from Sea.* (1613)

* To furnish a ship requires much trouble.

But to furnish a woman the charges are double.

John Manningham. *Diary*. p. 12. (1602)

* A man who wants to make himself a world of trouble

should get himself a ship and a woman, just those two.

Plautus. *Poenulus*. 1. 210. (c. 194 B.C.)

138. Gli uomini fanno la roba e le donne la conservano.

   * L'uomo porta e la donna dispensa. (Calabrese)

   Men get wealth, and women keep it.

      Thomas Fuller, *Gnomologia*. (1732)

   * Husbands can earn, but only wives can save.

      An English proverb

   * Every man who is high up loves to think he has done it all himself;
   and the wife smiles, and lets it go at that.

      James Matthew Barrie, *What Every Woman Knows*, act IV. (1908)

   * Many one blames their wife for their own unthrift.

      James Kelly, *Scottish Proverbs*. (1721)

   * The wife is the key of the house.

      Thomas Draxe, *Bibliotheca*. (1616)

   * La donna sapiente edifica la propria casa.

   ma la stolta la distrugge con le sue mani.

      Antico Testamento: Proverbi. 14:1. Garzanti

   Every wise woman buildeth her house:

   but the foolish plucketh it down with her hands.

      Old Testaments Proverbs. 14:1. King James Version

139. Chi ha molti soldi conta sempre.

   Chi ha una moglie bella canta sempre. (Napoletano)

   (He who has a lot of money is always counting;

   He who has a beautiful wife is forever singing).

   * Felice lo sposo di una donna virtuosa,

   il numero dei suoi giorni sarà raddoppiato.

      Scritti apocrifi: Ecclesiastico. 26:1. Edizioni Paoline

   Happy is the husband of a good wife;

   the number of his days will be doubled.

      Apocrypha: Ecclesiasticus. 26:1. Revised Standard Version - Catholic
      Edition

   * La grazia d'una donna è la gioia di suo marito,

   e il suo sapere gli dona vigore.

      Scritti apocrifi: Ecclesiastico. 26:13. Edizioni Paoline

The grace of a wife delighteth her husband
and her discretion will fatten his bones.

Apocrypha: Ecclesiasticus, 26:13. American Bible Society

* A good and virtuous wife is the most precious jewel of one's life.

Confucius, *The Analects*. (c. 500 B.C.) From Tehyi Hsieh, *Confucius Said It First*.

140. *Il buon marito fa la buona moglie.*

* La buona moglie fa il buon marito.

A good husband makes a good wife.

Robert Burton, *The Anatomy of Melancholy*, pt. III, sec. 3, member 4, subsec. 1. (1621)

* A good wife makes a good husband.

John Heywood, *Proverbs,* pt. II, ch. 8. (1546)

* Good wives and good plantations are made by good husbands.

Benjamin Franklin, *Poor Richard's Almanack*. (1736)

* A good Jack makes a good Gill.

John Ray, *English Proverbs*. (1670)

* The good Gill may mend the bad Jack.

Richard Brathwait, *History of Moderation*, p. 15. (1669)

* Chi ama la propria moglie ama se stesso.

Nuovo Testamento: Efesini, 5:28. Edizioni Paoline

He that loveth his wife loveth himself.

New Testament: Ephesians, 5:28. King James Version

* Parents ... should be affectionate toward each other.

Confucius, *The Analects*. (c. 500 B.C.) From Lin Yutang, *The Wisdom of Confucius*.

141. *Se la moglie pecca, non è il marito innocente.*

(If the wife sins, the husband is not innocent)

* Each husband gets the infidelity he deserves.

Zelda Popkin, *No Crime for a Lady*, p. 19. (1942)

* As the husband is, the wife is.

Lord Tennyson, *Locksley Hall*, 1.47. (1842)

* If you make your wife an ass, she will make you an ox.

Thomas Fuller, *Gnomologia*. (1732)

* The wife seldom rambles till the husband shows her the way.

Sir John Vanbrugh, *The Provoked Wife*, act V, sc. iv. (1698)

* It is their husbands' faults If wives do fall.

Shakespeare, *Othello*, act IV, sc. iii, 1. 87. (.1605)

142. La porta di dietro è quella che ruba la casa.

* Benedetta è quella casa che ha un sol battente.

The back door robs the house.

George Herbert, *Jacula Prudentum.* (1640)

* The postern door makes thief and whore.

Thomas Fuller, *Gnomologia.* (1732)

* A nice wife and a back door, do often make a rich man poor.

John Ray, *English Proverbs.* (1670)

* A light wife doth make a heavy husband.

Shakespeare, *The Merchant of Venice*, act V, sc. i. 1. 130. (1597)

143. Dove entra dote, esce libertà.

(Where dowry comes in, freedom goes out)

* Who wives for a dower resigns his own power.

An English proverb

* Stick to your class.

Agatha Christie, *The Tuesday Club Murders*, ch. 13. (1933)

* Marry above your match, and you get a master.

James Kelly, *Scottish Proverbs.* (1721)

* He that marries for wealth, sells his liberty.

George Herbert, *Jacula Prudentum.* (1640)

* Marry with your match.

John Clarke, *Paroemiologia.* (1639)

* According to the wise saying, choose one every way
as near as may be equal in birth and goods.

John Lyly, *Euphues: The Anatomy of Wit*, p. 150. (1579) Arber's reprint

* I accepted a dowry and lost an empire.

A Latin proverb

* If you wish to marry well, marry your equal.

Ovid, *Heroides*: Epistle ix, 1. 32. (c. 10 B.C.)

* I sold myself for a dowry.

Plautus, *Asinaria*, 1. 87. (c. 200 B.C.)

* Everyone ought to marry in one's own degree.

> Aeschylus, *Prometheus Bound*, 1. 887. (c. 470 B.C.)

144. *Il padrone di casa sono io; chi comanda è mia moglie.*

(I am the master of my house, but it is my wife who commands)

* In Italia comanda lui, in casa mia comando io.

(He rules Italy, but I am in command of my own house).

> Rachele Mussolini, *Epoca*, No. 1518, p. 11. November 10, 1979.
> Donna Rachele was referring to her husband, Benito Mussolini (1883-1945), Italian statesman.

* In their household it was the husband who wore the petticoats and the wife the trousers.

> Marcel Proust, *Sodome et Gomorrhe*, pt. I, p. 64. (1921)

* "Petticoat influence.. is a great reproach.

> Lord Byron, *Don Juan*, canto XIV, stanza 26. (1823)

* His wife "ruled the roast, " and in governing the governor, governed the province, which might thus be said to be under petticoat government.

> Washington Irving, *Knickerbocker's History of New York*, bk. IV, ch. 4. (1809)

* He would be quarter-master at home, if his wife would let him.

> Thomas Fuller, *Gnomologia*. (1732)

* He who has a wife has a master.

> James Kelly, *Scottish Proverbs*. (1721)

* As the good man says, so say we; but as the good woman says, so must it be.

> John Ray, *English Proverbs*. (1670)

* Hold your tongue, husband. and let me talk that have all the wit.

> John Ray, *English Proverbs*. (1670)

* In this place most master wear no breeches.

> Shakespeare, *King Henry VI*, Part II, act I, sc. iii, 1. 149. (1591)

145. *In casa non c'è pace, quando la gallina canta e il gallo tace.*

* Dove la donna domina e governa, ivi sovente la pace non sverna.

(There is no peace in the house, when the hen crows and the cock is silent).

* Wife a mouse, quiet house; wife a cat, dreadful that.

David Garrick, *The Irish Widow*, act I, sc. iii. (1772)

* Ill thrives that hapless family that shows

A cock that's silent, and a hen that crows;

I know not which lives more unnatural lives,

Obeying husbands, or commanding wives.

   Benjamin Franklin, *Poor Richard's Almanack.* (1734)

* It's a sad house where the hen crows louder than the cock.

   John Ray, *English Proverbs.* (1670)

* It is a silly flock where the ewe bears the bell.

   David Ferguson, *Scottish Proverbs.* (c. 1595)

* Trista è quella casa ove le galline cantano, e il gallo tace.

   John Florio, *Firste Fruites.* (1578)

They are sorry houses where the hens crow,

and the cock holds his peace.

   Florio, *ibid.*

* It is disgraceful for the wife

and not the man to rule the house.

   Euripides, *Electra*, 1. 932. (c. 413 B.C.)

146. *Dove la donna regna, la guerra infuria. (Siciliano)*

* Quando la donna regna, il diavolo governa.

(Where a woman reigns, war rages).

* Every man can rule a shrew save he that hath her.

   William Carew Hazlitt, *English Proverbs.* (1869)

* Oh! ye lords of ladies intellectual,

Inform us truly, have they not hen-peck'd you all?

   Lord Byron, *Don Juan*, canto I, stanza 22. (1818)

* If your wife command your purse,

she will certainly have the mastery in everything else.

   James Kelly, *Scottish Proverbs.* (1721)

* With what anxious strife,

What pain, we tug that galling load, a wife!

   William Congreve, *The Old Bachelor*, act V, sc.xv. (1693)

* He lives under the sign of the cat's foot.

He is hen-pecked, his wife scratches him.

   John Ray, *English Proverbs.* (1670)

* One had as good be nibbled to death by ducks,
or pecked to death by a hen.

> John Ray, *English Proverbs*. (1670)

* If you give your wife a yard, she'll take an ell.

> Thomas Dekker, *The Honest Whore*, pt. II, act II, sc. ii. (1630)

* Non darti in potere della donna, in modo da renderla tua dominatrice.

> *Scritti apocrifi: Ecclesiastico*, 9:2. Edizioni Paoline

Do not give yourself to a woman

so that she gains mastery over your strength.

> *Apocrypha: Ecclesiasticus*, 9:2. Revised Standard Version - Catholic Edition

147. *Tre cose cacciano l'uomo di casa: fumo, goccia, e femmina arrabbiata.*

Three things drive a man out of his house

- smoke, rain, and a scolding wife.

> *The Oxford Dictionary of English Proverbs*. (1948)

* There are three things which drive a man out of his house:

smoke, dripping, and a bad wife.

> Pope Innocent III (Giovanni Lotario dei conti di Segni) *De Contemptu Mundi*, pt. I, sec. 18. (c. 1210)

* Le risse della moglie sono un gocciolar continuo.

> *Antico Testamento: Proverbs*, 19:13. Diodati, tr.

The contentions of a wife are a continual dropping.

> *Old Testament Proverbs*, *19:13*. King James Version

* Meglio abitare in un angolo di soffitta,

che in comoda casa con donna bisbetica.

> *Antico Testamento: Proverbi*, 21:9. Edizioni Paoline

It is better to dwell in a corner of the housetop,

than with a brawling woman in a wide house.

> *Old Testament: Proverbs*, 21:9. King James Version

* Stillicidio noioso in giorno di pioggia e donna bisbetica sono tutt'uno.

> *Antico Testamento: Proverbi*, 27:15. Edizioni Paoline

A continual dropping in a very rainy day

and a contentious woman are alike.

> *Old Testament: Proverbs*, 27:15. King James Version

148. *Tra moglie e marito non mettere il dito.*

* Tra l'incudine ed il martello, man non metta chi ha cervello.
Don't interfere between husband and wife.

   Mario Hazon, *Grande Dizionario Inglese-Italiano, Italiano-Inglese*.
   (1974)

* What God has joined together no man shall ever put asunder:
God will take care of that.

   George Bernard Shaw, *Getting Married*. (1908)

* When the two have been united, no man may separate them.

   William Scarborough, *Chinese Proverbs*. (1875)

* Is it for me to stir up strife between them, and put
as 'twere my finger betwixt the bark and tree?

   Sir Walter Scott, *The Monastery*, ch. 4. (1820)

* Let none but Him who rules the thunder
Put this man and woman asunder.

   Jonathan Swift, *Marriage Service from His Chamber Window*. (c.
   1745)

* Of all actions of a man's life his marriage
 does least concern other people,
yet of all actions of our life
'tis most meddled with by other people.

   John Selden, *Table Talk, Marriage*. (1689)

* Put not your hand between the rind and the tree.

   David Ferguson, *Scottish Proverbs*. (c. 1595)

   It were folly for me
To put my hands between the bark and the tree.

   John Heywood, *Proverbs*, pt. II, ch. 2. (1546)

* Perciò non divida l'uomo quello che Dio ha unito.

   Nuovo Testamento: Matteo, 19:6. Edizioni Paoline

What therefore God hath joined together,
let not man put asunder.

   New Testament: Matthew, 19:6. King James Version

149. *Doglia di moglie morta dura fino alla porta.*

* Il dolore della moglie è come il dolore del gomito.
(Sorrow for a dead wife lasts as far as the door).

* Grief for a dead wife, and a troublesome guest...

79

Continues to the threshold, and there is at rest.

    Benjamin Franklin, *Poor Richard's Almanack*. (1734)

* 'Tis a sweet sorrow to bury an outrageous wife.

    Thomas Fuller. *Gnomologia*, (1732)

* Here lies my wife: here let her lie!

Now she's at rest, and so am I.

    John Dryden, *Epithaph for his wife*. (c. 1700)

150. *Chi perde moglie e un quattrino, ha gran perdita del quattrino.*

He that loses his wife and a farthing has a great loss of his farthing.

    John Ray, *English Proverbs*. (1670)

* Every man has two good days with his wife -

the day he marries her, and the day he buries her.

    Charles Haddon Spurgeon, *John Ploughman's Talk*, ch. 17. (1869)

* The death of wives, and the standing of sheep

is the best thing ever came a poor man's gate.

    James Kelly, *Scottish Proverbs*. (1721)

* He that loses his wife and sixpence, has lost a tester (i.e., sixpence).

    John Ray, *English Proverbs*. (1670)

* A dead wife's the best goods in a man's house.

    John Ray, *English Proverbs*. (1670)

* Who throws away a tester and a mistress, loses sixpence.

    George Farquhar, *Love and Bottle*, act II, sc. 1. (1699)

151. *Chi non ha figli, non sa cosa sia amore.*

He that has no children knows not what is love.

> John Ray, *English Proverbs*. (1670)

* The world has no such flower in any land,

And no such pearl in any gulf the sea,

As any babe on any mother's knee.

> Algernon Charles Swinburne. *Poems*: Pelagius, stanza 2. (1904 Edition)

* Where children are not, heaven is not.

> Algernon Charles Swinburne, *A Song of Welcome*. (1871)

* A mother's pride, a father's joy.

> Sir Walter Scott. *Rokeby*. canto III, stanza 15. (1813)

* They say barnes are blessings.

> Shakespeare. *All's Well that Ends Well*, act I, sc. iii. 1. 28. (1602)

* What is sweeter than one's own children?

> Cicero, *Post Reditum ad Quirites*, ch. 1, sec. 2. (c. 57 B.C.)

* Begetting children is a delightful duty.

> Plautus, *Miles Gloriosus*, 1. 682. (c. 200 B.C.)

* Childreh are the most sweet things to have.

> Menander, *The Girl Who Gets Her Hair Cut*, 1. 691. (c. 300 B.C.)

152. *Il corvo pensa che i suoi pulcini siano i più belli.*

* All'orsa paiono belli i suoi orsacchiotti. (Toscano)

* Ogni scarafaggio è bello per mamma sua. (Napoletano)

The crow thinks her own birds fairest.

> John Ray, *English Proverbs*. (1670)

* There's only one pretty child in the world, and every mother has it.

> An English proverb

* Everyone thinks his own owl a falcon.

> A Flemish proverb

* De Lord can' make no chil'en so black

but what dey mother loves 'em.

> Mark Twain (Samuel Langhorne Clemens), *A True Story*. (1875)

* My babe so beautiful! it thrills my heart

With tender gladness.

    Samuel Taylor Coleridge, *Frost at Midnight*, 1. 48.(c. 1798)

* The owl thinks all her young ones beauties.

    Thomas Fuller, *Gnomologia*. (1732)

* Where yet was ever found a mother

Who'd give her booby for another?

    John Gay, *Fables*, pt. I, The Mother, the Nurse, and the Fairy. (1727)

* I ... like the foolish crow,

Believe my black brood swans.

    Philip Massinger, *The Unnatural Combat*, act III, sc. ii. (1639)

* Every crow thinks her own bird fairest.

    Robert Burton, *The Anatomy of Melancholy*, pt. III, sec. 1, member 2, subsec. 3. (1621)

* The crow thinks her own birds fairest in the wood.

    John Heywood, *Proverbs*, pt. II, ch. 4. (1546)

153. *Figli piccoli, guai piccoli; figli grandi, guai grandi.*

    * Figli piccoli, dolor di testa; figli grandi, dolor di cuore.

(Little children, little trouble; big children, big trouble).

* Children are a constant torment and nothing more.

    Leo Nikolaevich Tolstoy, *The Kreutzer Sonata*, ch.. 4. (1890)

* Children, when little make parents fools; when great, mad.

    Thomas Fuller, *Gnomologia*. (1732)

* Children suck the mother, when they are young;

and the father, when grown up.

    Thomas Fuller, *Gnomologia*. (1732)

* Children are certain cares, but uncertain comforts.

    John Ray, *English Proverbs*. (1670)

* Children when they are little make parents fools,

when they are great they make them mad.

    George Herbert, *Jacula Prudentum*. (1640)

154. *Chi vuol esser mal servito,tenga assai famiglia.*

    * Un figlio, nessun figlio; due figli, pochi figli;

tre figli, giusti figli; quattro figli, troppi figli; cinque figli

con la madre, sei diavoli contro il padre.

(He who wants to be ill served, let him have a large family).

* When you've got one, you may run,

When you've got two, you may go,

But when you've got three, you must stop where you be.

   An English proverb

* He that has a wife and children,

must not sit with his fingers in his mouth.

   Thomas Fuller, *Gnomologia*. (1732)

* Wife and children are hostages given to Fortune.

   Thomas Fuller, *Gnomologia*. (1732)

* For what secures the civil life

But pawns of children, and a wife?

   Samuel Butler, *Hudibras*, pt. III, canto 1,1. 809. (1678)

* Wife and children are bills of charges.

   John Ray, *English Proverbs*. (1670)

* He that has a wife and children, wants not business.

   George Herbert, *Jacula Prudentum*. (1640)

* He that has a wife and children has given hostages to Fortune.

   Francis Bacon, *Essays: Of Marriage and Single Life*. (1597)

* There is nothing more wretched than a father,

except another father of more children.

   Menander. *Fragments*: fragment 656. (c. 300 B.C.)

* The more children you have the more griefs you have.

   Aesop. *Fables*: *The Dove and the Crow*. (c. 570 B.C.)

155. *Basta un padre a governare cento figli,*

   e cento figli non bastano a governare un padre.

   * Un padre e una madre bastano a cento figli,

cento figli non bastano a un padre e a una madre.

One father is enough to govern one hundred sons,

but not a hundred sons one father.

   George Herbert, *Jacula Prudentum*. (1640)

   * One father supports ten children better than ten children one father.

   A German proverb

156. *Son tutti figli d'un ventre, ma non tutti d'una mente.*

   (Calabrese)

83

* Tutte le dita non son pari.

(They are all children of the same mother,

but not all are of the same mind).

* The same tree may bear sweet and sour fruit.

> Justus Doolittle, *Chinese Vocabulary*. (1872)

* Good wombs have borne bad sons.

> Shakespeare, *The Tempest*, act I, sc. ii, 1. 120. (1611)

* Every like is not the same.

> Shakespeare, *Julius Caesar*, act II, sc. ii, 1. 128. (1599)

* Many a good cow had an evil calf.

> John Heywood, *Proverbs*, pt. I, ch. 10. (1546)

* The children of Mercurie and of Venus

Been in hir wirking ful contrarious;

Mercurie loveth wisdom and science,

And Venus loveth ryot and dispence.

> Geoffrey Chaucer, *The Canterbury Tales*: The Wife of Bath's
> Prologue, 1. 697. (c. 1388)

* For god it woot, that children ofte been

Unlyk her worthy eldres hem bifore.

> Geoffrey Chaucer, *The Canterbuty Tales*: The Clerk's Tale, 1. 99. (c.
> 1388)

* Com'esser può di dolce seme amaro.

(From sweet seed may come forth bitter [fruit]).

> Dante, *La Divina Commedia: Paradiso*, canto VIII, 1. 93. (c. 1320)

157. *In ogni gregge c'è una pecora nera.*

* Di padre santolotto, figlio diavolotto.

* Dalla rosa nasce la spina. (Calabrese)

There's a black sheep in every flock.

> An English proverb

* The father a saint, the son a devil.

> Henry George Bohn, *Handbook of Proverbs*. (1855)

* Nobody's family can hang out the sign, "Nothing the matter here."

> A Chinese saying

* Black sheep dwell in every fold.

> William Schwenck Gilbert, *H.M.S. Pinafore*, act II. (1878)

* There's a scabby sheep in every flock.
    John Glyde, Jr., *A Norfolk Garland*, p. 150. (1872)
* Kate, the "black sheep" of the family.
    George John Whyte-Melville, *Kate Coventry*, ch. 13. (1856)
* The rose has its thorn, the peach its worm.
    Thomas Chandler Haliburton (Sam Slick), *Wise Saws*, ch. 26. (1843)
* We have no rose without its thorn.
    Thomas Jefferson, *Letter to Mrs. Cosway*. (1786)
* He that has no fools, knaves, nor beggars in his family.
was begot by a flash or lightning.
    Thomas Fuller, *Gnomologia*. (1732)
* Roses have thorns. and silver fountains mud.
    Shakespeare, *Sonnets*: sonnet XXXV. (1609)
* Of every ordre some shrewe is, parde.
    Geoffrey Chaucer, *The Canterbury Tales*: The Canon's Yeoman's
    Tale, 1. 442. (c. 1387)

158. *Basta un matto per casa.*

(One fool in a house is enough)

* Two fools in a house are too many by a couple.
    Thomas Fuller, *Gnomologia*. (1732)
* Two fools in one house is over many.
    David Ferguson, *Scottish Proverbs*. (c. 1595)
* Chi genera uno stolto si procura fastidi,
e il padre d'uno sciocco non gioirà.
    Antico Testamento: Proverbi, 17:21. Edizioni Paoline
He that begetteth a fool doeth it to his sorrow: and
the father of a fool hath no joy.
    Old Testament: Proverbs, 17:21. King James Version

159. *Da puledro scabbioso, anche cavallo prezioso.*

* Gattini sventati fanno gatti posati.
A ragged colt may make a good horse.
    Henry George Bohn, *A Handbook of Proverbs*. (1855),
    John Ray, *English Proverbs*. (1670)
* Wanton kittens may make sober cats.
    Henry George Bohn, *Handbook of Proverbs*. (1855)

* A wild colt may become a sober horse.

Thomas Fuller, *Gnomologia*. (1732)

* Wanton kittens may make sober old cats.

Thomas Fuller, *Gnomologia*. (1732)

* A ragged colt may prove a good horse.

James Kelly, *Scottish Proverbs*. (1721) George Chapman, *Eastward Hoe*, act V, sc. i. (1605)

* Of a ragged colt comes a good horse.

John Heywood. *Proverbs*, pt. I. ch. 11. (1546)

* How different is the man you are from the child you were.

Ovid, *Heroides*: Epistle ix. 1. 24. (c. 10 B.C.)

160. *La gallina nera fa l'uovo bianco.*

* Di uovo bianco spesso pulcin nero.
* Anche tra le spine nascono le rose.

A black hen lays a white egg.

John Ray, *English Proverbs*. (1670)

* Among the thorns the rose is born.

A Latin proverb

* O! the wonderful works of nature,

that a black hen should lay a white egg.

Jonathan Swift, *Polite Conversation, Dialogue I*. (c. 1738)

* A black hen may bring forth white eggs.

Thomas Draxe, *Bibliotheca*. (1616)

* From most sharp thorns ... spring most sweet flowers.

George Pettie, *Petite Pallace*, p. 91. (1576)

161. *Figlio troppo accarezzato non fu mai ben allevato.*

* I figli si baciano quando dormono. (Meridionale)

(A child who was fondled too much was never brought up right).

* A spoilt child never loves its mother.

Sir Henry Taylor, *Notes from Life*, p. 123. (1885)

* Mother's darlings make but milk-sop heroes.

Thomas Fuller, *Gnomologia*. (1732)

* The more you rub a cat on the rump,

the higher she sets her tail.

John Ray, *English Proverbs*. (1678)

* Let not a child sleep upon bones. (i.e., upon one's lap)

John Ray, *English Proverbs*. (1670)

* A child may have too much of his mother's blessing.

John Ray, *English Proverbs*. (1670) Ray explains,

"Mothers are oftentimes too tender and fond of their children,

who are ruined and spoiled by their cockering and indulgence."

* He that cockers his child, provides for his enemy.

George Herbert, *Jacula Prudentum*. (1640)

* A man may have too much of his mother's blessing.

John Clarke, *Paroemiologia*. (1639)

162. La madre pietosa fa la figlia tignosa.

(A soft-hearted mother spoils her daughter).

* Light-heel'd mothers make leaden-heeled daughters.

Thomas Fuller, *Gnomologia*. (1732)

* A bleat cat makes a proud mouse.

James Kelly, *Scottish Proverbs*. (1721) Kelly comments, "When parents and masters are too mild and easy, it makes their children and servants too saucy and impertinent.

* A light-heel'd mother makes a heavy-heel'd daughter.

John Ray, *English Proverbs*. (1670)

163. Chi ha un porco solo lo fa grasso,

e chi ha un figlio solo lo fa matto. (Veneziano)

* Cavallo ingrassato tira calci.

He that has but one hog, makes him fat,

and he that has but one son, makes him a fool.

John Ray, *English Proverbs*. (1670)

* Colt in de barley-patch kick high.

Joel Chandler Harris, *Uncle Remus: Plantation Proverbs*. (1880)

* Give a child till he craves,

and a dog while his tail does wave,

and you'll have a fair dog, but a foul knave.

John Ray, *English Proverbs*. (1670)

* He that has one hog, makes him fat;

and he that has one son, makes him a fool.

George Herbert, *Jacula Prudentum*. (1640)

164. I fanciulli diventano uomini.

* Al nascer la spina porta la punta in cima.

Boys will be men.

> Thomas Fuller, *Gnomologia*. (1732)

* The thorn comes forth with its point .forwards.

> George Herbert, *Jacula Prudentum*. (1640)

* The Child is father of the Man.

> William Wordsworth, *My Heart Leaps up When I Behold*. (1802)

* The childhood shows the man,

As morning shows the day.

> John Milton, *Paradise Regained*, bk. IV, 1. 220. (1671)

* It early pricks that will be a thorn.

> John Ray, *English Proverbs*. (1670)

* Youth, what man's age is like to be, does show;

We may our ends by our beginnings know.

> Sir John Denham, *On Prudence*, 1. 225. (1650)

* As they say, boys will be men one day.

> Randle Cotgrave, *French-English Dictionary*. (1611)

* It pricks betimes that will be a good thorn.

> John Heywood, *Proverbs*, pt. II, ch. 9. (1546)

* Fin da fanciullo l'uomo è riconosciuto da' suoi atti.

> *Antico Testamento: Proverbi*, 20:11. Diodati, tr.

Even a child is known by his doings.

> *Old Testament: Proverbs*, 20:11. King James Version

165. L'albero si deve piegare quando è giovane.

* Finchè la pianta è tenera, bisogna drizzarla.

* Albero vecchio non si piega più.

(Bend the tree while it is young).

* Just as the twig is bent, the tree's inclined.

> Alexander Pope, *Moral Essays: Epistle I, To Lord Cobham*, 1. 150. (1734)

* A colt you may break, but an old horse you can never.

> Thomas Fuller, *Gnomologia*. (1732)

* Rule youth well, and age will rule itself.

> James Kelly, *Scottish Proverbs*. (1721)

* Old and tough, young and tender.

    John Ray, *English Proverbs*. (1678)

* Best to bend while 'tis a twig.

    John Ray, *English Proverbs*. (1670)

* Young twigs are sooner bent than old trees.

    John Lyly, *Euphues and His England*, p. 314. (1580) Arber's reprint

* The tender youth of a child is like

the tempering of new wax, apt to receive any form.

    John Lyly, Euphues: *The Anatomy of Wit*, p. 37. (1579) Arber's reprint

* The wildest colts make the best horses,

if only they get the proper breaking and training.

    Themistocles (c. 490 B.C.) From Plutarch, *Lives: Themistocles*, ch. 2, sec. 5.

* Castiga il tuo figliuolo mentre vi è ancora della speranza.

    Antico Testamento: Proverbi, 19:18. Diodati, tr.

Chasten thy son while there is hope.

    Old Testament: Proverbs, 19:18. King James Version

* Abitua il fanciullo alla buona condotta,

e pur invecchiando, non l'abbandonerà

    Antico Testamento: Proverbi, 22:6. Edizioni Paoline

Train up a child in the way he should go:

and when he is old, he will not depart from it.

    Old Testament: Proverbs, 22:6. King James Version

166. *Chi ben ama, ben castiga.*

* Mazze e panelli fanno i figli belli. (Meridionale)

(He who loves well, punishes well).

* If you love your child don't spare the rod.

William Scarborough, *Chinese Proverbs*. (1875)

167. *Chi risparmia il bastone non vuole bene ai figli. (Napoletano)*

* Panelli senza mazze fanno i figli pazzi. (Meridionale)

(He who spares the rod does not love his children).

* Spare the rod and spoil the child, as the Good Book says.

    Mark Twain (Samuel Langhorne Clemens), *Tom Sawyer*, ch. 1. (1876)

* I have a brother to whom my poor mother spared the rod,

and who ... has turned out but a spoilt child.

William Makepeace Thackeray, *The Newcomes*, ch. 3. (1855)

* Spare the rod and spoil the child.

John Ray, *English Proverbs*. (1670)

* They spare the rod and spoil the child.

Ralph Venning, *Mysteries and Revelations*, p. 5. (1649)

* Love is a boy by poets styl'd;

Then spare the rod, and spoil the child.

Samuel Butler, *Hudibras*, pt. II, canto 1,1. 843. (1664)

* That sour tree of knowledge - now a birch.

Thomas Hood, *The Irish Schoolmaster*, stanza 6. (c. 1840)

* Let your'child's first lesson be obedience,

and the second be what you will.

Benjamin Franklin, *Poor Richard's Almanack*. (1739)

* Love well, whip well.

Benjamin Franklin, *Poor Richard's Almanack*. (1733)

* Birchen twigs break no ribs.

John Clarke, *Paroemiologia*. (1639)

* Beget them with pleasure, and bring them up with pain.

George Pettie, *Petite Pallace*, p. 67. (1576)

* Sferza e correzione sono sempre opportune.

Scritti apocrifi: Eccesiastico, 22:6. Edizioni Paoline

Stripes and corrections are at all times wisdom.

Apocrypha: Ecclesiasticus, 22:6. Oesterley, tr.

* Chi risparmia la verga odia suo figlio,

ma chi lo ama lo corregge.

Antico Testamento: Proverbi, 13:24. Garzanti

He that spareth his rod hateth his son:

but he that loveth him chasteneth him betimes.

Old Testament: Proverbs, 13:24. King James Version

168. *E' meglio che piangano i fanciulli e non i vecchi.*

Better children weep than old men.

John Heywood, *Proverbs*, pt. II, ch. 7. (1546)

* Better that bairns weep than bearded men.

Sir Walter Scott, *Tales of a Grandfather*, ch. 32. (1827)

* He that will not use the rod on his child,

his child shall be used as a rod on him.

Thomas Fuller, *The Holy and Profane State*, bk. I, ch. 5. (1642)

* Woe to the house where there is no chiding.

George Herbert, *Jacula Prudentum*. (1640)

* Better a little chiding than a great deal of heartbreak.

Shakespeare, *The Merry Wives of Windsor*, act V, sc. iii, 1. 11. (1601)

* Unruly children make their sire stoop.

Shakespeare, *King Richard II*, act III, sc. iv, 1. 30. (1595)

* Chi ama suo figlio, gli farà provare la sferza,

perché più tardi possa rallegrarsi di lui.

Scritti apocrifi: Ecclesiastico, 30:1. Edizioni Paoline

He who loves his son will whip him often,

in order that he may rejoice at the way he turns out.

Apocrypha: Ecclesiasticus, 30:1. Revised Standard Version - Catholic Edition

* Evils not punished at the beginning grow greater.

Aesop, *Fables*: The Boy and His Mother. (c.570 B.C.)

* La verga e la correzione danno saggezza,

ma il fanciullo abbandonato a se stesso

sarà la vergogna di sua madre.

Antico Testamento: Proverbi, 29:15. Edizioni Paoline

The rod and reproof give wisdom:

but a child left to himself

bringeth his mother to shame.

Old Testament: Proverbs, 29:15. King James Version

169. *Avanti la morte non lice chiamar alcun felice.*

(It is not proper to call anyone happy before his death).

* Praise a fair day at night.
  An English proverb

* Praise not the day before night.
  Thomas Fuller, *Gnomologia.* (1732)

* Praise day at night, and life at end.
  George Herbert, *Jacula Prudentum.* (1640)

* La vita el fin, e '1 dì loda la sera.

(The end praises the life, and the evening the day)
  Francesco Petrarca, *Il Canzoniere*, canzone I, stanza 2, 1. 11. (c. 1345)

* No man can be called happy before he is dead and buried.
  Ovid, *Metamorphoses*, bk. III. 1. 136. (c. A.D. 7)

* Prima della fine non proclamar felice alcuno.
  Scritti apocrifi: Ecclesiastico, 11:28. Edizioni Paoline

Call no man happy before his death.
  Apocrypha: Ecclesiasticus, 11:28. Revised Standard Version - Catholic Edition

* Count no man happy until he die.
  Euripides, *The Daughters of Troy*, 1. 510. (c. 415 B.C.)

170. *L'allegria è d'ogni male il rimedio universale.*

* Gente allegra Iddio l'aiuta. (Toscano)

(Mirth is the universal remedy for every ill).

* Mirth is the medicine of life,
  It cures its ills and calms its strife.
  David Kin, *Dictionary of American Proverbs.* (1955)

* Of cheerfulness, or of good temper,
  the more it is spent, the more of it remains.
  Ralph Waldo Emerson, *The Conduct of Life:Considerations by the Way.* (1860)

* Cheerfulness is the principal ingredient in the composition of health.
  Arthur Murphy. *The Apprendice.* act II, sc. iv. (1756)

* A man of gladness seldom falls into madness.

James Howell. *English Proverbs*. (1659)

* Il cuore allegro giova come una medicina.
  Antico Testamento: Proverbi, 17:22. Diodati, tr.

A merry heart doeth good like a medicine.
  Old Testaments Proverbs, 17:22. King James Version

171. *L'allegria fa bello il viso.*

(Mirth makes the face beautiful).

* Cheerfulness is just as natural to the heart
of a man in strong health as colour to his cheek.
  John Ruskin, *Modern Painters*, vol. IV, pt. V, ch. 19. (1856)

* The heart's mirth does make the face fair.
  Book of Merry Riddles, proverb 54. (1629)

* The joy of the heart makes the face merry.
  Thomas Draxe, *Bibliotheca*. (1616)

* The joy of the heart fairly colours the face.
  John Davies of Hereford, *The Scourge of Folly*, p. 46. (1611)

* The happiness of the heart causes a fair color in the face.
  John Florio, *Firste Fruites*. (1578)

* Il cuore dell'uomo cambia il suo volto, sia in bene e sia in male.
  Scritti apocrifi: Ecclesiastico, 13:25. Garzanti

A man's heart changes his countenance, either for good or for evil.
  Apocrypha: Ecclesiasticus, 13:25. Revised Standard Version - Catholic Edition

* Il cuore allegro abbellisce la faccia.
  Antico Testamento: Proverbi, 15:13. Diodati, tr.

A merry heart maketh a cheerful countenance.
  Old Testament: Proverbs, 15:13. King James Version

172. *Il riso fa buon sangue.*

* Chi ride leva un chiodo alla bara. (Toscano)

(Laughter engenders good blood)

* Laugh and grow fat.
  Mario Hazon, *Grande Dizionario Inglese-Italiano, Italiano-Inglese*. (1974)

* Happiness is beneficial for the body.
  Marcel Proust, *Remembrance of Things Past: The Past Recaptured*. (c. 1921)

* Laffing is the sensation of feeling good all over.

  Josh Billings (Henry Wheeler Shaw), *Sayings: Laffing*. (1858)

* Singing will make a man laugh,

And laughing long life does bring.

  Thomas D'Urfey, *Pills to Purge Melancholy: old Simon the King*. (1719)

* 'Tis a good thing to laugh ... and if a straw can

tickle a man, it is an instrument of happiness.

  John Dryden, *Essays*, vol. II. p. 133. (c. 1700)

* When shall we sup together, and laugh and be fat?

  Ben Jonson, *Every Man Out of His Humour*, act III, sc. i. (1599)

* Hang sorrow, care'll kill a cat.

  Ben Jonson, *Every Man in His Humour*, act I, sc. iii. (1598)

* Let care kill a cat, we'll laugh and grow fat.

  The Shirburn Ballads, p. 91. (1585)

173. La musica ricrea lo spirito.

(Music refreshes the soul).

* Music's the medicine of the mind.

  John Logan, *Danish Ode*. (c. 1788)

* Music's force can tame the furious beast.

  Matthew Prior, *Solomon on the Vanity of the World*, bk. II, 1. 67. (1718)

* As some to church repair,

Not for the doctrine, but the music there.

  Alexander Pope, *An Essay on Criticism*, pt. II, 1. 141. (1711)

* Music has charms to soothe a savage breast,

To soften rocks, or bend a knotted oak.

  William Congreve, *The Mourning Bride*, act I, sc. i, 1. 1. (1697)

* Music is said to be the rejoicing of the heart.

  John Florio, *Firste Fruites*. (1578)

* O [music] sweet and healing medicine of trouble.

  Horace, *Odes*, bk. I, ode xxxii, 1. 14. (c. 23 B.C.)

* Music is most sovereign because ... rhythm and har

find their way into the secret places of the soul.

  Plato, *The Republic*, bk. III, ch. 12. (c. 375 B.C.)

174. Chi canta,i suoi mali spaventa.

(He who sings scares away his troubles)

* The schoolboy ... whistling aloud to keep his courage up.
    Robert Blair, *The Grave*, pt. I, 1. 58. (1743)

* I am ... afraid ... but I'll sing that I may seem valiant.
    John Dryden, *Amphitryon*, act II, sc. i. (1690)

* Whistling to keep myself from being afraid.
    John Dryden, *Amphitryon*, act III, sc. iii. (1690)

* He who sings scares away his woes.
    Miguel de Cervantes, *Don Quixote de la Mancha*, pt. I, ch. 22. (1605)

* Black care will be lessened by sweet song.
    Horace, *Odes*, bk. IV, ode xi, 1. 35. (c. 23 B.C.)

175. E' meglio il cuor felice che la borsa piena.

* Non si vive di solo pane.
A happy heart is better than a full purse.
    Henry George Bohn, *Handbook of Proverbs*. (1855)

* Man is a creature who live not by bread alone.
    Robert Louis Stevenson, *Virginibus Puerisque*, pt. I, ch. 2. (1881)

* Man does not live by bread alone.
    Ralph Waldo Emerson, *The Sovereignty of Ethics*. (1875)

* It is neither wealth, nor splendor, but tranquillity
and occupation, which give happiness.
    Thomas Jefferson, *Letter to Mrs. A. S. Marks*. (1788)

* Non di solo pane vivrà l'uomo.
    Nuovo Testamento: Matteo, 4:4. Edizioni Paoline
Man shall not live by bread alone.
    New Testament: Matthew, 4:4. King James Version

* A happy life consists in tranquillity of mind.
    Cicero, *De Natura Deorum*, bk. I, sec. 20. (c.45 B.C.)

* Happiness comes from the health of the soul.
    Aeschylus, *Eumenides*, 1. 535. (c. 458 B.C.)

* L'uomo vive non soltanto di pane.
    Antico Testamento: Deuteronomio, 8:3. Garzanti
Man doth not live by bread only.
    Old Testament: Deuteronomy, 8:3. King James Version

176. Chi si contenta gode.

* Chi non ha gran voglie è ricco.

(He who is content is happy).

* A contented mind is a perpetual feast.

    Mario Hazon, *Grande Dizionario Ing!ese-Italiano, Italiano-Inglese.* (1974)

* Content makes poor men rich; discontent makes rich men poor.

    Benjamin Franklin, *Poor Richard's Almanack.* (1749)

* Who is rich? He that rejoices in his portion.

    Benjamin Franklin, *Poor Richard's Almanack.* (1744)

* Content is happiness.

    Thomas Fuller, *Gnomologia.* (1732)

* Poor and content is rich, and rich enough.

    Shakespeare, *Othello*, act III, sc. iii, 1. 172. , (1605)

* Enough is as good as a feast.

    John Heywood, *Proverbs*, pt. I, ch. 11. (1546)

* Contentatevi di quel che avete.

    Nuovo Testamento: Ebrei, 13:5. Edizioni Paoline

Be content with such things as ye have.

    New Testament: Hebrews, 13:5. King James Version

* Contented with your lot, you will live wisely.

    Horace, *Epistles*, bk. I, epistle 10,1.44. (c. 20 B.C.)

* To be contented with what we have is the greatest
and most certain wealth of all.

    Cicero, *Paradoxa*, bk. VI, sec.3 (c. 45 B.C.)

177. Il mondo è di chi se lo piglia.

* Chi vuol vivere e star bene prenda il mondo come viene.

(The world belongs to him who knows how to take it).

* The world is as you take it.

    An English proverb

* Take the world as it is, not as it ought to be.

    A German proverb

* Happiness grows at our own firesides, and is not to
be picked up in strangers' gardens.

    Douglas William Jerrold, *Jerrold's Wit: Happiness.* (c. 1840)

* Man is the artificer of his own happiness.

    Henry David Thoreau, *Journal*, January 21, 1838.

* Il mondo è un bel libro, ma poco serve a chi non lo sa leggere.

(The world is a beautiful book, but it is of little use

to him who does not know how to read it).

    Carlo Goldoni, *Pamela*, act I, sc. xiv. (1760)

* I consider the world as made for me, not me for the world.

It is my maxim therefore to enjoy it while I can.

    Tobias Smollett, *Roderick Random*, ch. 45. (1748)

* The gown is hers that wears it; and the world is his who enjoys it.

    John Ray, *English Proverbs*. (1670)

* Make much of what you have.

    John Clarke, *Paroemiologia*. (1639)

* Take all things as they come and be content.

    John Davies of Hereford. *The Scourge of Folly*, p. 296. (c. 1611) John Heywood, *Proverbs*, pt.I. ch.4. (1546)

178. Felice non è chi d'esser non sa.

(He is not happy who does not know himself so)

* Ask yourself whether you are happy.

    John Stuart Mill, *Autobiography*, ch. 5. (1873)

* I am not happy at all unless I am happier than I know.

    Alexander Smith, *Dreamthorp*, ch. 7. (1863)

* Happiness is nothing if it is not known.

    Samuel Johnson, *The Idler*, No. *80*. (1758)

* No man can enjoy happiness without thinking that he enjoys it.

    Samuel Johnson, *The Rambler*, No. 150. August 24, 1751

* He is happy, that knows not himself to be otherwise.

    Thomas Fuller, *Gnomologia*. (1732)

* No one is happy who does not think himself so.

    Publilius Syrus, *Sententiae*. (c. 43 B.C.)

179. Il tempo buono viene una volta sola.

* Quando il sol ti splende, non ti curar della luna.

(Happiness comes only once).

* Happiness passes everyone once in life.

    A German proverb

* Happiness has wings.

 A German proverb

* To fill the hour - that is happiness.

 Ralph Waldo Emerson, *Essays*: Second Series, Experience. (1844)

* Happiness too swiftly flies.

 Thomas Gray, *On a Distant Prospect of Eton College*, stanza 10. (1742) .

* There is an hour wherein a man could be happy

all his life could he find it.

 George Herbert, *Jacula Prudentum*. (1651)

* Where the sun shines, the moon has nought to do.

 Thomas Draxe, *Bibliotheca*. (1616)

* No happiness lasts for long.

 Seneca, *Agamemnon*, 1. 928. (c. A.D. 60)

* What is given by the gods more desirable than a happy hour?

 Catullus, *Odes*, ode lxii, 1. 30. (c. 57 B.C.)

* Happiness is ... transient.

 Euripides, *Phoenissae*, 1. 558. (c. 420 B.C.)

180. *Al Taborre ognuno accorre: il Calvario è solitario.*

 (Everybody runs to the Tabor while the Calvary is solitary).

* A sorrow that's shared is but half a trouble,

But a joy that's shared is a joy made double.

 An English proverb

* Knock and the world knocks with you,

Boost and you boost alone.

 An English saying

* One can endure sorrow alone, but it takes two to be glad.

 Elbert Hubbard, *A Thousand and One Epigrams*. (1911)

* Grief can take care of itself, but to get the full value

 from joy you must have somedody to divide it with.

 Mark Twain (Samuel Langhorne Clemens), *Following The Equator*, vol. II, *Pudd'nhead Wilson's New Calendar*, ch. 12. (1897)

* Laugh, and the world laughs with you;

Weep, and you weep alone;

For the sad old earth must borrow its mirth,

But has trouble enough of its own.

Ella Wheeler Wilcox, *Solitude*, stanza 1. (1883)

* All who joy would win

Must share it, —Happiness was born a twin.

Lord Byron, *Don Juan*, canto II, stanza 172. (1819)

* Rallegratevi con quelli che sono allegri.

Nuovo Testamento: Romani, 12:15. Diodati, tr.

Rejoice with them that do rejoice.

New Testament: Romans, 12:15. King James Version

181. A chi troppo ride gli duole il cuore.

(He who laughs too much has an aching heart).

* I shall laugh my bitter laugh.

   Epitaph on Nikolai Gogol's tombstone. (1852)

* If I laugh at any mortal thing,

'Tis that I may not weep.

   Lord Byron, *Don Juan*, canto IV, stanza 3. (1821)

* I laugh at everything, for fear of having to cry.

   Pierre de Beaumarchais, *Le Barbier de Seville*, act I, sc. ii. (1775)

* I am forced to make myself laugh that I may not cry.

Samuel Richardson, *The History of Clarissa Harlowe*, letter 84. (1748)

* Anche ridendo il cuore può esser triste.

   Antico Testamento: Proverbi, 14:13. Garzanti

Even in laughter the heart is sorrowful.

   Old Testament: Proverbs, 14:13. King James Version

182. Non c'è gioia senza noia.

No joy without alloy.

   Henry George Bohn, *Handbook of Proverbs*. (1855)

* From the fount of joy's delicious springs

Some bitter o'er the flowers its bubbling venom flings.

   Lord Byron, *Childe Harold's Pilgrimage*, canto I, stanza 82. (1812)

* Joy must have sorrow.

   Johann Wolfgang von Goethe, *Faust*, pt. I, sc. x. (1806)

* We have ... no pleasure without alloy.

   Thomas Jefferson, *Letter to Mrs. Cosway*. (1786)

* No joy without annoy.

   John Clarke, *Paroemiologia*. (1639)

* No pleasure without pain.

   Michel Eyquem de Montaigne, *Essays*, bk. III, ch. 3. (1595)

* From the heart of this fountain of delights wells up some bitter taste.

   Lucretius, *De Rerum Natura*, bk. IV, 1. 1133. (c. 45 B.C.)

183. Non c'è dolce senza amaro.

(There is no sweet without bitter)

* Life to have its sweets must have its sours.

John Masefield, *The Widow in the Bye Street*, pt. IV, stanza 25. (1912)

* Every sweet has its sour.

Ralph Waldo Emerson, *Essays*: First Series, Compensation. (1841)

* Sweetest nut hath sourest rind.

Shakespeare, *As You Like It*, act III, sc. ii, 1. 115. (1600)

* Every sweet with soure is tempred. .

Edmund Spenser, *Amoretti*: sonnet XXVI. (1595)

* The tree that bears the sweetest fruit, has a sour sap.

John Lyly, Euphues: *The Anatomy of Wit*, p. 79. (1579) Arber's reprint

* The sweets are mixed with the bitters.

Martial, *Epigrams*, bk. XII, No. 34. (A.D. c. A.D.40-c. 104)

184. *Dopo il dolce viene l'amaro.*

* Dopo il contento vien il tormento.

After the sweet comes the sour.

Mario Hazon, *Grande Dizionario Inglese-Italiano, Italiano-Inglese.* (1974)

* Pleasure seems sweet, but proves a glass of bitters.

David Garrick, *She Stoops to Conque*r, Epilogue. (1773)

* Grief often treads upon the heels of pleasure.

Benjamin Franklin, *Poor Richard's Almanack.* (1734)

* Sweet in the on taking, but sour in the off putting.

James Kelly, *Scottish Proverbs.* (1721)

* Never pleasure without repentance.

John Ray, *English Proverbs.* (1670)

* God send us joy, for sorrow will come fast enough.

John Clarke, *Paroemiologia.* (1639)

* Wo after gladnesse

Geoffrey Chaucer, *The Canterbury Tales:* The Knight's Tale, 1. 1983. (c. 1386)

* Sorrow follows joy.

A Latin proverb

185. *Per un giorno di gioia, n'abbiamo mille di noia.*

* Un'ora di contento sconta cent'anni di tormento.

(For one day of joy, we have a thousand days of grief).

* Every inch of joy has an ell of annoy.
   An English proverb
* Short pleasures, long pains.
   Thomas Fuller, *Gnomologia*. (1732)
* Short pleasure, long lament.
   John Ray, *English Proverbs*. (1670)
* All instances of pleasure have a sting in the tail.
   Bishop Jeremy Taylor, *Holy Living*, ch. 2, sec. 1. (1650)
* Pleasure will be paid, one time or another.
   Shakespeare, *Twelfth Night*, act II, sc. iv, 1. 72. (1599)
* Eighty odd years of sorrow have I seen,
And each hour's joy wrecked with a week of teen.
   Shakespeare, *King Richard III*, act IV, sc. i, 1. 96. (1593)
* For every dram of pleasure, an .ounce of pain;
for every inch of mirth, an ell of moan.
   John Lyly *Euphues: The Anatomy of Wit*, p. 107. (1579) Arber's
   reprint
* For every pint of honey, a gallon of gall.
   George Pettie, *Petite Pallace*, p. 237. (1576)

186. *Non ha il dolce a caro chi provato non ha l'amaro.*
   (He who has not tasted the bitter cannot appreciate the sweet).
* He who has not tasted the bitterest of life's bitters
can never appreciate the sweetness of life's sweets.
   A Chinese proverb
* Sweet is pleasure after pain.
   John Dryden, *Alexander's Feast*, 1. 58. (1697)
* The bitter goes before the sweet. Yes, and for as
much as it does, it makes the sweet the sweeter.
   John Bunyan, *The Pilgrim's Progress*, pt. II. (1684)
* He deserves not the sweet that will not taste the sour.
   James Howell, *English Proverbs*. (1659)
* The bitter past, more welcome is the sweet.
   Shakespeare, *All's Well that Ends Well*, act V, sc. iii, 1. 334 (1602)
* As by the bad is the good known,
so by the sour is the sweet better discerned.

John Florio, *Firste Fruites*. (1578)

* Each joy is made more pleasant

by first tasting some sour sops of sorrow.

George Pettie, *Petite Pallace*, p. 61. (1576)

* For how might ever sweetnesse have be knowe

To him that never tasted bitternesse?

Geoffrey Chaucer, *Troilus and Criseyde*, bk. I, l. 638. (c. 1385)

187. Quel che fu duro a patire, è dolce a ricordare.

That which was bitter to endure, may be sweet to remember.

Thomas Fuller, *Gnomologia*. (1732)

* Sorrows remembered sweeten present joy.

Robert Pollok, *The Course of Time*, bk. 1,1.464. (1827)

* 'Tis sweet to think on what was hard to endure.

Robert Herrick, *Satisfaction for Suffering*. (1648)

* The remembrance of past sorrow is joyful.

John Clarke, *Paroemiologia*. (1639)

* All these woes shall serve

For sweet discourses in our time to come.

Shakespeare, *Romeo and Juliet*, act III, sc. v, 1. 52. (1595)

* That which was hard to bear is sweet to remember.

Seneca, *Hercules Furens*, 1. 656. (c. A.D. 60)

* The memory of past woes is pleasant.

Cicero, *De Finibus*, bk. II, ch. 32, sec. 105.(c. 46 B. C.)

188. Ricordarsi il ben doppia la noia.

(The remembrance of happiness doubles the pain).

* This is truth the poet sings,

That a sorrow's crown of sorrow is remembering happier things.

Lord Tennyson, *Locksley Hall*, 1. 75. (1842)

* Of joys departed

Not to return, how painful the remembrance!

Robert Blair, *The Grave*, 1. 109. (1743)

* The memory of happiness makes misery woeful.

Thomas Fuller, *Gnomologia*. (1732)

* The remembrance of pleasure doubles our pain.

Michel Eyquem de Montaigne, *Essays*, bk. II, ch. 12. (1580)

* For of fortunes sharpe adversitee
The worste kinde of infortune is this,
A man to have ben in prosperitee ,
And it remembren, when it passed is.

>   Geoffrey Chaucer, *Troilus and Crisyde*, bk. III, 1. 1625. (c. 1385)

* Nessun maggior dolore,
che ricordarsi del tempo felice nella miseria.
(There is no greater pain
than to recall a happy time in misery).

>   Dante, *La Divina Commedia: Inferno*, canto V, 1. 121. (c. 1312)

189. *Tutto il male non viene per nuocere.*

* Non c'è male senza bene.
* Spesso da un gran male nasce un gran bene.
(Misfortunes do not always come to harm).
* Good can come from evil.

>   An English proverb

* Every cloud has a silver lining.
The Oxford Dictionary of English Proverbs. (1948)
* There's a silver lining
Through the dark cloud shining.

>   Lena Guilbert Ford, *Keep the Home Fires Burning.* (1915)

* One may not doubt that somehow Good
Shall come of Water and or Mud.

>   Rupert Brooke, *Heaven.* (1913)

* There's a silver lining to every cloud.

>   William Schwenck Gilbert, *The Mikado*, act II. (1885)

* We trust that somehow good
Will be the final goal of ill.

>   Lord Tennyson, *In Memoriam*, pt. LIV, stanza 1. (1850)

* Every evil [has] its good.

>   Ralph Waldo Emerson, *Essays: First Series, Compensation.* (1841)

* There is no evil without its compensation.

>   Seneca, *Ad Lucilium*, epistle lxix, sec. 4. (c. A.D. 64)

190. *Non c'è cosa così cattiva che non sia buona a qualche cosa.*

Nothing so bad as not to be good for something.

Henry George Bohn, *Handbook of Proverbs*. (1855)

* There is so much good in the worst of us,

And so much bad in the best of us.

Attributed to Governor Edward Wallis Hoch (Kansas). (1849 - 1925)

* There are two kinds of people on earth to-day,

Just two kinds of people, no more, I say.

Not the good and the bad, for 'tis well understood

That the good are half bad, and the bad are half good.

Ella Wheeler Wilcox, *To Lift or to Lean*. (c. 1890)

* In men whom men condemn as ill

I find so much of goodness still,

In men whom men pronounce divine

I find so much of sin and blot.

Joaquin Miller (Cincinnatus Hiner), *Byron*. (1871)

* Nothing so bad in which there is not something of good.

John Ray, *Adagia.Hebraica*. (1678)

* There is some soul of goodness in things evil,

Would men observingly distill it out.

Shakespeare, *King Henry V*, act IV, sc. i, 1.4. (1599)

* Non è male alcuno nelle cose umane

che non abbia congiunto seco qualche bene.

(There is no bad in human affairs

that has not some good connected with it).

Francesco Guicciardini, *Storia d'Italia*. (1530)

* Good things are mixed with bad, bad things with good.

A Latin proverb

191. *Non è mai mal per uno che non sia ben per un altro.*

* Non pianse mai uno che non ridesse un altro.

(What is bad for one may be good for another).

* One man's fault is another man's lesson.

Henry George Bohn, *Handbook of Proverbs*. (1855)

* One man's justice is another's injustice; ...

one man's wisdom another's folly.

Ralph Waldo Emerson, *Essays*: First Series, Circles. (1841)

* Good for the liver may be bad for the spleen.
    Thomas Fuller, *Gnomologia*. (1732)
* That which is good for the back is bad for the head.
    John Ray, *English Proverbs*. (1678)
* The folly of one man is the fortune of another.
    Francis Bacon, *Essays: Of Fortune*. (1597)
* Whatsoever is some where gotten is some where lost.
    Francis Bacon, *Essay:. Of Seditions and Troubles*. (1597)
* One man's gain is another man's loss.
    A Latin proverb

No one gains except by another's loss.
    Seneca, *De Ira*, bk. II, ch. 8. (c. A.D. 55)
* Gain cannot be made without another's loss.
    Publilius Syrus, *Sententiae*. (c.43 B.C.)

192. La morte del lupo è la sanità della pecora.
    * Se uno non muore, l'altro non gode. (Toscano)
    * Morte tua, vita mia.

The death of the wolf is the health of the sheep.
    John Florio, *Firste Fruites*. (1578)
* The death of the wolf is life to the lambs.
    Arthur Christopher Benson, *Along the Road*, p. 270. (1913)
* One man's breath is another man's death.
    Thomas Fuller, *Gnomologia*. (1732)
* The death of the wolves is the safety of the sheep.
    George Herbert, *Jacula Prudentum*. (1640)
* The life of the wolf is the death of the lamb.
    John Clarke, *Paroemiologia*. (1639)
* One man's meat is another man's poison.
    An English proverb
* What's one man's poison, signor,

Is another's meat or drink.
    Francis Beaumont and John 'Fletcher, *Love's Cure*, act III, sc. ii.
    (c. 1613)
* What is food to one, is bitter poison to another.
    Lucretius, *De Rerum Natura*, bk. IV, 1. 637. (c. 45 B.C.)

193. *I pensieri fanno mettere i peli canuti.*

(Worries make one grow gray hair).

* Fretting cares make gray hairs.

An English jingle from the Latin proverb:

"Care grows gray hair".

* It is not work that kills, but worry.

Dinah Maria Mulock Craik, *Young Mrs.Jardine*, bk. III, ch. 9. (1879)

* Care to our coffin adds a nail, no doubt;

But every grin so merry draws one out.

Peter Pindar (John Wolcot) , *Expostulatory Odes*, ode 15. (1789)

* 'Tis a folly to fret; grief's no comfort.

John Ray, *English Proverbs*. (1678)

* Care killed a cat.

Shakespeare, *Much Ado About Nothing*, act V, sc. i, 1. .135. (1598)

* Care is no cure, but rather corrosive.

Snakespeare, *King Henry VI*, Part I, act III, sc. iii, 1. 3. (1591)

* Le preoccupazioni portano la vecchiaia prima del tempo.

Scritti apocrifi: Ecclesiastico, 30:24. Garzanti

Worry will make you old before your time.

Apocrypha: Ecclesiasticus, 30:24. Good News Bible

194. *Cento carri di pensieri non pagheranno un'oncia di debito.*

* Cent'ore di malinconia non pagano un quattrino di debito.

(A hundred cart loads of worries will not pay an ounce of debt).

* A hundred years of regret

Pay not a farthing of debt.

Charles Haddon Spurgeon, *John Ploughman's Talk*, ch. 12. (1869)

* A pound of care will not pay an ounce of debt.

Thomas Fuller, *Gnomologia*. (1732)

* Sorrow will pay no debt.

John Ray, *English Proverbs*. (1670)

* A hundred load of thought will not pay one of debt.

George Herbert, *Jacula Prudentum*. (1640)

* A pound of care pays not a dram of debt.

Thomas Dekker, *The Shoemaker's Holiday*, act III, sc. v. (1599)

195. *Mal comune, mezzo gaudio. (Toscano)*

* Aver compagni al duol scema la pena.

(A common sorrow is half a joy).

* A sorrow shared is a sorrow halved.

> Mario Hazon, *Grande Dizionario Inglese-Italiano, Italiano-Inglese*. (1974)

* If we share our troubles we halve them.

> Patricia Wentworth, *Miss Silver Deals with Death*, p. 17. (1943)

* Miserey certainly does enjoy the society of accomplices.

> O. Henry (William Sydney Porter), *The Day We Celebrate*. (1911)

* Two in distress
Make sorrow less.

> Henry George Bohn, *Handbook of Proverbs*. (1855)

* Misery loves company.

> Henry David Thoreau ,*Journal*, September 1, 1851.

* Company in distress
Make the sorrow less.

> Thomas Fuller, *Gnomologia*. (1732)

* In misery it is great comfort to have a companion.

> John Lyly, *Euphues: The Anatomy of Wit*, p. 96. (1579) Arber's reprint

* One pain is lessen'd by another's anguish.
One desperate grief cures with another's languish.

> Shakespeare, *Romeo and Juliet*, act I, sc. ii, 1.47. (1595)

* Grief best is pleased with grief's society.

> Shakespeare, *The Rape of Lucrece*, 1. 1111. (1594)

* It is sweet to mingle tears with tears.

> Seneca, *Agamemnon*, 1. 664. (c. A.D. 60)

196. *Non c'è sì piccola casetta che non abbia la sua crocetta.*

* Ognuno porta la sua croce.

* Ad ognuno par più grave la sua croce.

(There is no house, however small, without its own small cross).

* Every man has his own cross to bear.

> An English proverb

* We all has to have our troubles.

> Mark Twain (Samuel Langhorne Clemens), *Huckleberry Finn*, ch. 1.3. (1884)

* Every man must bear his own burden.

    Charles Kingsley, *Westward Ho!,* ch. 26. (1855)

* Every heart has its own ache.

    Thomas Fuller, *Gnomologia.* (1732)

* Each cross has its inscription.

    John Ray, *English Proverbs.* (1670)

* Everyone thinks his own sack heaviest.

    George Herbert, *Jacula Prudentum.* (1640)

* Everyone finds his own burden heavy.

    Randle Cotgrave, *French-English Dictionary.* (1611)

* Ciascuno porterà il suo proprio peso.

    Nuovo Testamento: Galati, 6:5. Diodati, tr.

Every man shall bear his own burden.

    New Testament: Galatians, 6:5. King James Version

197. *I gran dolori sono muti.*

(Great griefs are silent).

* No words suffice the secret soul to show,

For Truth denies all eloquence to Woe.

    Lord Byron, *The Corsair*, canto III, stanza 22. (1813)

* In all the silent manliness of grief.

    Oliver Goldsmith, *The Deserted Village*, 1. 384. (1770)

* Grief that given way to verses, is not very lamentable.

    Thomas Fuller, *Gnomologia.* (1732)

* Grief loathes words.

    Thomas Dekker, *The Honest Whore*, pt. I, act I, sc. i. (1604)

* Our passions are most like the floods and streams,

The shallow murmur, but the deep are dumb.

    Sir Walter Ralegh, *Sir Walter Ralegh to the Queen*, stanza 1. (c. 1599)

* Striving to tell his woes, words would not come;

For light cares speak, when mighty griefs are dumb.

    Samuel Daniel, *The Complaint of Rosamond*, stanza 114. (1592)

* Light griefs speak, the great are dumb.

    Seneca, *Hippolytus*, 1. 607. (c. A.D. 60)

198. *Il piangere è un sollievo.*

(Weeping is a comfort).

* Tears are summer showers to the soul.

   Alfred Austin, *Savonarola*, act IV. (1881)

* To weep is to make less the depth of grief.

   Shakespeare, *King Henry VI*, Part III, act II, sc. i, 1. 85. (1591)

* Tears lighten the soul.

   Seneca, *Ad Lucilium*, epistle xcix, sec. 16. (c. A.D. 60)

* Grief is sated and relieved by tears.

   Ovid, *Tristia*, bk. IV, elegy 3. 1. 38. (c. A.D. 2O)

199. *Chi nasce è sempre bello; chi si sposa è sempre buono; chi muore è sempre santo. (Napoletano)*

    * Quando nascono son tutti belli;

quando si maritano son tutti buoni;

quando muoiono son tutti santi.

(He who is born is always beautiful;

he who marries is always good;

he who dies is always a saint).

200. *Meglio un asino vivo che un dottore morto.*

    (Better a living ass than a dead doctor).

    * A live dog is better than a dead lion.

        Mario Hazon, *Grande Dizionario Inglese-Italiano, Italiano-Inglese.* (1974)

    * I'd rather fight flies in a boarding house

Than fill Napoleon's grave.

        O. Henry (William Sydney Porter), *Chanson de Boheme.* (1894)

    * E' meglio un cane vivo che un leone morto.

        Antico Testamento: Ecclesiaste. 9:4. Edizioni Paoline

A living dog is better than a dead lion.

        Old Testament: Ecclesiastes, 9:4. King James Version

201. *C'è un posto per tutti sotto il sole.*

    (There's a place for everyone under the sun).

    * This world's an inn, all travellers are we;

And this world's goods th' accomodations be.

        Benjamin Franklin, *Poor Richard's Almanack.* (1744)

    * The world's a wide place.

        Jonathan Swift, *Polite Conversation*, Dialogue II, (c. 1738)

    * The world is a wide parish.

        James Howell, *English Proverbs.* (1659)

202. *Bisogna vivere e lasciar vivere.*

    * O bene o male, tutti dobbiamo vivere.

    * Vivi, e lascia vivere.

One must live and let live.

Tobias Smollett, *Sir Launcelot Greaves*, ch. 16. (1762)

* There is enough in the world for everyone to have

plenty to live on happily and to be at peace with his neighbors.

Harry S. Truman, *Memoirs*, vol. I. *Years of Decisions*, preface. (1955)

* Live and let others live.

A Dutch proverb

* Live and let live.

Johann Cristoph Friedrich von Schiller, *Wallensteins Lager*, act IV, 1. 106. (1798) John Ray, *English Proverbs*. (1678)

203. *Ad ogni cosa c'è rimedio fuorchè alla morte.*

* Tutto s'accomoda eccetto l'osso del collo. (Calabrese)

There is a remedy for all things except stark death.

John Ray, *English Proverbs*. (1678)

* There is no cure for birth and death save to enjoy the interval.

George Santayana, *Soliloquies in England: War Shrines*. (1922)

* There is a remedy for everything except death.

Miguel de Cervantes, *Don Quixote de la Mancha*, pt. II, ch. 4). (1615)

* A tutto è rimedio eccetto che alla morte.

John Florio, *Firste Fruites*. (1578)

Unto all is remedy, except into death.

Florio, *ibid.*

* Against the evil of death there is no medicine in the gardens.

A medieval Latin proverb

204. *La vita non è tutta rose.*

Life is not a bed of roses.

An English proverb

* Life isn't all beer and skittles.

Thomas Hughes, *Tom Brown's Schooldays*, pt. I, ch. 2. (1857)

* Life is made up of marble and mud.

Nathaniel Hawthorne, *The House of the Seven Gables*, ch. 2. (1851)

* Life is a series of surprises.

Ralph Waldo Emerson, *Essays*: First Series, Circles. (1841)

* The web of our life is of a mingled yarn, good and ill together.

Shakespeare, *All's Well that Ends Well*, act I, sc. iii, 1. 83. (1602)

* Life is a mixture of grief and joy.

Phaedrus, *Fables*. bk. IV, fable 17. (c. A.D. 8)

205. *La vita è una continua battaglia.*

(Life is a continuous battle)

* As the wind is ... mortal life.

A moan, a sigh, a sob, a storm, a strife.

Sir Edwin Arnold. *The Light of Asia*. bk. 111.1.23. (1879)

* Life' s a long tragedy this globe the stage.

Isaac Watts, *Epistle to Mitio*. pt. I,1. 1. (c. 1748)

* We are born crying, live complaining, and die disappointed.

Thomas Fuller, *Gnomologia*. (1732)

* It is a misery to be born, a pain to live, a trouble to die.

St. Bernard of Clairvaux, *De Consideratione*, pt. V. (c. 1130)

* Life ... is a battle.

Marcus Aurelius, *Meditations*, bk. II, sec. 17. (c. A.D. 174)

* Life is a struggle.

Euripides, *Suppliants*, 1. 550. (c. 421 B.C.)

Non è un servizio militare quello che l'uomo fa sulla terra?

Antico Testamento: Giobbe, 7:1. Garzanti

The life of man on earth is a warfare.

Old Testament: Job, 7:1. The Vulgate Version

206. *Il tempo vola.*

* Ad ora ad ora vola tutto il tempo.

Time flies away without delay.

John Ray, *English Proverbs*. (1670)

* For though we slepe or wake, or rome, or ryde,

Ay fleeth the tyme, it nil no man abyde.

Geoffrey Chaucer, *The Canterbury Tales: The Clerk's Tale*, 1. 62. (c. 1388)

* Nothing is swifter than the years,

Ovid, *Metamorphoses*, bk. X, 1. 520. (c. A.D. 7)

* While I am speaking, the hour flies.

Ovid, *Amores*, bk. I, elegy 11,1. 15. (c. 13 B.C.)

* Time flies away.

Virgil, *Georgics*, bk. 111,1. 284. (c. 30 B.C.)

207. *La vita è breve.*

(Life is brief).

* Ed è subito sera.

 (And suddenly it's evening).

    Salvatore Quasimodo, *Ed è Subito Sera.* (1942)

* Life is too short ...

'Twill soon be dark.

    Ralph Waldo Emerson, *Poems*: To J. W.(1847)

* The world's a bubble, and the life of man less than a span.

    Francis Bacon, *The World.* (c. 1628)

* Life's but a span.

    Shakespeare, *Othello*, act II, sc. iii, 1. 73. (1605)

* The time of life is short.

    Shakespeare, *King Henry IV*, Part I, act V, sc. ii, 1. 81. (1597)

* Quanto è il tempo nostro? E' quanto una punta d'ago.

(How long is our life? As long as a tip of a needle).

    Santa Caterina da Siena, *Pensieri e Sentenze.* 3. (c. 1375) From F. Palazzi e S. Spaventa Filippi, *Il Libro dei Mille Savi.* (1955)

208. *La vita è breve e l'arte è lunga.*

Life is short and art is long.

    The Oxford Dictionary of English Proverbs. (1948)

    Seneca, *De Brevitate Vitae*, sec. 1. (c. A.D. 49)

* Art is long, and Time is fleeting.

    Henry Wadsworth Longfellow, *A Psalm of Life*, stanza 4. (1839)

* Life is short, the art long, opportunity fleeting,

experience treacherous, judgment difficult.

    Hippocrates, *Aphorisms*, sec. 1, No.1. (c. 400 B.C.)

The father of medicine is referring to the art of healing.

209. *La vita è un affacciarsi al balcone. (Calabrese)*

(Life is but a brief appearance on a balcony).

* The longest life is but a parcel of moments.

    Henry George Bohn, *Handbook of Proverbs.* (1855)

* Life is a stroll upon the beach.

    Henry David Thoreau, *My Life Is a Stroll Upon the Beach*, stanza 1. (1849)

* A man's life's no more than to say "One".

Shakespeare, *Hamlet*, act V, sc. ii, 1. 74. (1600)

* Life is but a moment in time.

Plutarch, *Moralia: On the Education of Children*, sec. 13. (c. A.D. 100)

* Che cosa è la vostra vita?

Un vapore che appare per poco e poi svanisce.

Nuovo Testamento: Giacomo, 4:14. Garzanti

What is your life? It is even a vapour, that appeareth

for a little time, and then vanisheth away.

New Testament: James, 4:14. King James Version

* Ricordati che la mia vita è un vento.

Antico Testamento: Giobbe, 7:7. Diodati, tr.

Remember that my life is wind.

Old Testaments Job, 7:7. King James Version

210. *La vita è un sogno.*

(Life is a dream).

* Contessa, che è mai la vita?

E' l'ombra d'un sogno fuggente.

(Countess, what on earth is life?

It is the shadow of a fleeting dream).

Giosuè Carducci, *Poesie*: Jaufrè Rudel. (1871)

* Life is but an empty dream.

Henry Wadsworth Longfellow, *A Psalm of Life*, stanza 1. (1839)

* Life is an empty dream.

Robert Browning, *Paracelsus*, pt. II. (1835)

* All we see or seem

Is but a dream within a dream.

Edgar Allan Poe, *A Dream Within a Dream*. (1827)

* What is life? Life is a dream.

Pedro Calderón de la Barca, *Life Is a Dream*, act II, 1. 1195. (c. 1640)

* Life's but a walking shadow.

Shakespeare, *Macbeth*, act V, sc. v, 1. 23. (1606)

* Life is. a dream.

Michel Eyquem de Montaigne, *Essays*, bk. II, ch. 12. (1580)

211. *La vita passa, e la morte viene.*

John Florio, *Firste Fruites*. (1578)

Life does pass, and death does come.

Florio, *ibid.*

* Hatch, match, and dispatch.

James Payn, *By Proxy*, ch. 19. (1878)

* Ships that pass in the night, and speak each other in passing,

Only a signal shown and a distant voice in the darkness;

So on the ocean of life we pass and speak one another,

Only a look and a voice; then darkness again and a silence.

Henry Wadsworth Longfellow, *Tales of a Wayside Inn*, pt. III, *The Theologian's Tale: Elizabeth*, IV. (1873)

* Live your life, do your work, then take your hat.

Henry David Thoreau, *A Week on the Concord and Merrimack Rivers*. (1849)

* La vita fugge ... e la morte vien dietro.

(Life flees ... and death follows close behind).

Francesco Petrarca, *Il Canzoniere*, sonetto CCXXIX. (c. 1348)

212. *Ognuno ha il proprio destino.*

> Every man has his lot.
>> Thomas Fuller, *Gnomologia.* (1732)

> * In your breast are the stars of your fate.
>> Johann Christoph Friedrich von Schiller, *Piccolomini*, act II, sc. vi. (1799)

> * Sua ventura ha ciascuno dal dì che nasce.

> (Every man is born with his destiny).
>> Francesco Petrarca, *Il Canzoniere*, sonetto XXXV. (c. 1350)

213. *Finchè uno ha denti in bocca non sa mai quel che gli tocca. (Toscano)*

> * Quel che non è stato, può essere.

> (No living man shall ever know his destiny).

> * Hands of invisible spirits touch the strings ...

> And play the prelude of our fate.
>> Henry Wadsworth Longfellow, *The Spanish Student*, act I, sc. iii. (1843)

> * None knows what will happen to him before sunset.
>> Thomas Fuller, *Gnomologia.* (1732)

> * There is a divinity that shapes our ends.
>> Shakespeare, *Hamlet*, act IV, sc. ii, 1, 10. (1600)

> *Non sapete ciò che sarà domani.
>> *Nuovo Testamento: Giacomo*, 4:14. Diodati, tr.

> Ye know not what shall be on the morrow.
>> *New Testament: James*, 4:14. King James Version

> * It is uncertain what the evening may bring forth.
>> Livy, *History*, bk. XLV, sec. 8. (c. 8 B.C.)

> * Non gloriarti del domani, perché non sai cosa partorirà l'oggi.
>> *Antico Testamento: Proverbi*, 27:1. Garzanti

> Boast not thyself of to morrow;

> for thou knowest not what a day may bring forth.
>> Old Testament: *Proverbs*, 27:1. King James Version

214. *Fino alla morte non si sa la sorte.*

> * Si sa dove si nasce; non si sa dove si muore. (Calabrese)

(Until death comes, no one knows his destiny).

* A man's destiny is always dark.

> George Herbert, *Jacula Prudentum*. (1651)

* O God! that one might read the.book of fate!

> Shakespeare, *King Henry IV*, Part II, act III, sc. i, 1.45. (1598)

* The lottery of my destiny

Bars me the right of voluntary choosing.

> Shakespeare, *The Merchant of Venice*, act II, sc. i, 1. 15. (1597)

215. *Che sarà sarà. (Motto of the Duke of Bedford)*

What shall be, shall be.

> John Heywood, *Proverbs*, pt. II, ch. 1. (1546)

* What doctrine call you this,

"Che sarà sarà," what will be, shall be?

> Christopher Marlowe, *The Tragical History of Doctor Faustus*, act I, sc. i. (Published in 1604)

216. *Quel che ha da essere, sarà.*

What is to be will be.

> O. Henry (William Sydney Porter), *Tobin's Palm*. (1906)

* Whan a thing is shapen, it shal be.

> Geoffrey Chaucer, *The Canterbury Tales*: *The Knight's*, 1. 608. (c. 1386)

* Whatever happens at all happens as it should.

> Marcus Aurelius, *Meditations*, bk. IV, sec. 10. (c. A.D. 174)

* What is to come, shall come.

> Aeschylus, *Agamemnon*, 1. 1240. (c. 458 B.C.)

217. *Il destino non lo cambia nessuno. (Calabrese)*

* Quel che è destinato mancar non può.

(No man can change his destiny).

* La Forza del Destino.

(The Power of Destiny) Title of an opera by Giuseppe Verdi.

> Libretto by Francesco Maria Piave. (1862)

* The fated will happen.

> A Gaelic proverb

* No man can make his own hap.

> James Kelly. *Scottish Proverbs*. (1721) David Ferguson. *Scottish Proverbs*. (1595)

* What is decreed must be.

  Shakespeare. *Twelfth Night*. act I, sc. v. 1. 329. (1599)

* The Fates rule over men.

  Juvenal, *Satires*: satire IX, 1. 32. (c. A.D. 120)

* Nothing can win fate.

  Ovid, *Tristia*, bk. III. elegy 6, 1. 18. (c. A.D. 10)

* Fate is stronger than anything.

  Euripides. *Alcestis*, 1. 962. (c. 438 B.C.)

218. *Nessuno può sfuggire al proprio destino.*

  (No one can escape his own destiny)

* Who shall shut out Fate?

  Sir Edwin Arnold. *The Light of Asia*, bk. 111,1. 336. (1879) :

* No flying from fate.

  Thomas Fuller, *Gnomologia*. (1732)

* Shunless destiny.

  Shakespeare, *Coriolanus*, act II, sc. ii, 1. 116. (1608)

* L'uomo il suo destin fugge di rado.

  (Rarely does man escape his destiny)

  Ludovico Ariosto, *Orlando Furioso*, canto XVIII, stanza 58. (1532)

* Inevitable fate.

  Virgil, *Aeneid*, bk. VIII, 1. 334. (c. 19 B.C.)

* There is no escape from it [fate] .

  Sophocles, *Antigone*, 1. 950. (c. 441 B.C.)

* No man may escape his destined lot.

  Herodotus, *History*, bk. I, ch. 91. (c. 445 B.C.)

* No one has ever escaped his destiny.

  Homer, *Iliad*, bk. VI, 1. 488. (c. 850 B.C.)

* Not even Hercules ... escaped his fate.

  Homer, *Iliad*, bk. XVIII, 1. 117. (c. 850 B.C.)

219. *Chi ha da esser impiccato non sarà mai annegato.*

* Chi ha da morir di forca puo ballar sul fiume.

* (He who has to be hanged shall never be drowned).

* He got out of the water ... not being born to be drowned.

  Daniel Defoe, *Colonel Jacque*, ch. 7. (1723)

* You can turn nobody from his destined end.

Jean de La Fontaine, *Fables*, bk. IX, fable 7. (1678)

* He that is born to be hanged shall never be drowned.

John Ray, *English Proverbs*. (1670)

* He hath no drowning mark upon him;

his complexion is perfect gallows.

Shakespeare, *The Tempest*, act V, sc. i, 1. 32. (1611)

220. *A quel che vien dal ciel non c'è riparo. (Toscano)*

(What must happen, shall happen regardless).

* Fate is a sea without a shore.

Algernon Charles Swinburne, *Hymn to Proserpine*. (1866)

* There is no armor against fate.

James Shirley, *The Contention of Ajax and Ulysses*, sc. iii. (1659)

* 'Tis vain to quarrel with our destiny.

Thomas Middleton, *A Trick to Catch the Old One*, act IV, sc. iv. (1607)

* What fates impose, that men must needs abide;

It boots not to resist both wind and tide.

Shakespeare, *King Henry VI*, Part III, act IV, sc. iii, 1. 58. (1591)

* Che giova nelle Fata dar di cozzo?

(Or what use is it to fight against the Fates?)

Dante, *La. Divina Commedia: Inferno*, canto IX, 1. 97. (c. 1312)

* No one shall alter Fate's decree.

Euripides, *Hercules Furens*, 1. 311. (c. 420 B.C.)

221. Muor giovane colui che al cielo è caro.

Whom the gods love dies young.

> Lord Byron, *Don Juan*, canto IV, stanza 12. (1821)

> Plautus, *Bacchides*, 1. 816. (c. 190 B. C.) Menander, *The Double Deceiver*, fragment 125. (c. 300 B.C.)

* Heaven gives its favourites early death.

> Lord Byron, *Childe Harold's Pilgrimage*, canto IV, stanza 102. (1818)

* The good die first,

And they whose hearts are dry as summer dust,

Burn to the socket.

> William Wordsworth, *The Excursion*, bk. I. (1814)

* The good die early, and the bad die late.

> Daniel Defoe, *Character of the Late Dr. S. Annesley*. (1715)

* Those that God loves do not live long.

> George Herbert, *Jacula Prudentum*. (1615)

222. Di giovani ne muoiono molti; di vecchi non ne scampa nessuno.

* I giovani possono morir presto,

ma i vecchi non possono campar molto.

Of young men die many; of old men escape not any.

> John Ray, *English Proverbs*. (1670)

* Young men may die, but old must die.

> Thomas Fuller, *Gnomologia*. (1732)

* Old men go to death; death comes to young men.

> George Herbert, Jacula Prudentum. (1640)

* There is but this difference between the death

of old men and young men;

that old men go to death, and death comes to young men.

> Francis Bacon, *Apothegms*, apothegm 119. (1624)

* May not Young men die as well as old?

> Shakespeare, *The Taming of the Shrew*, act II, sc. i, 1. 393. (1594)

223. Così tosto muore il capretto come la capra.

(As soon as the goat dies so does the kid).

* Death devours lambs as well as sheep.
  Thomas Fuller, *Gnomologia*. (1732)

* As soon as comes the lamb's skin to the market as the old sheep's.
  John Ray, *English Proverbs*. (1670)

* As soon goes the young lamb's skin to the market as the old ewe's.
  John Heywood, *Proverbs*. pt. II, ch. 4. (1546)

224. *Se vuoi vivere sano e lesto, fatti vecchio un po' più presto.*

   (If you want to live a healthy and fast life, become old early).

   * An old young man will be a young old man.
     Benjamin Franklin, *Poor Richard's Almanack*. (1735)

   * Be old betimes, that thou may'st long be so.
     Thomas Fuller, *Gnomologia*. (1732)

   * Old young and old long.
     John Ray, *English Proverbs* (1670)

   * They who would be young when they are old,
     must be old when they are young.
     John Ray, *English Proverbs*. (1670)

   * He that would be well old, must be old betimes.
     George Herbert, *Jacula Prudentum*. (1640)

   * Become old early if you want to stay old long.
     Cicero, Cato Maior *De Senectute*, ch. 10, sec. 32. (c. 44 B.C.)

225. *Presto maturo, presto marcio.*

   * Quel che presto matura, poco dura.
     Early ripe, early rotten.
     Thomas Fuller, *Gnomologia*. (1732)

   * Soon grass, soon hay.
     A Dutch proverb

   * So wise so young, they say, do never live long.
     Shakespeare, *King Richard III*, act III, sc. i, 1. 79. (1593)

   * Soon ripe, soon rotten.
     John Heywood, *Proverbs*, pt. I, ch. 10. (1546); A Latin proverb

   * Those who ripen early die young.
     Quintilian, *De Istitutio Oratoria*, bk. VI, ch. 2, sec. 10. (c. A.D. 93)

   * Precocious youth is a sign of premature death.

Pliny The Elder, *Natural History*, bk. VII, sec. 51. (c. A.D. 77)

226. *Si muore una volta sola.*

(We die but once).

* A man cannot die more than once.

Frederick Marryat. *Olla Podrida*, ch. 12. (1840)

* Men die but once.

Charles Lamb, *John Woodvil*, act II. sc. ii. (1802)

* With great submission I pronounce,

That people die no more than once.

Matthew Prior, *Turtle and Sparrow*. (1708)

* It is the lot of man but once to die.

Francis Quarles, *Emblems*, bk. V, emblem 7. (1635)

* A man can die but once.

Shakespeare, *King Henry IV*, Part II, act III, sc. ii, 1. 250. (1598)

227. *Tutti dobbiamo morire.*

(We all must die).

* That we shall die, we know.

Shakespeare, *Julius Caesar*, act III, sc. i, 1. 99. (1599)

* Death will have his day.

Shakespeare, *King Richard II*, act III, sc. ii, 1. 41. (1595)

* We know we must die.

Petronius, *Satyricon*, sec. 72. (c. A.D. 60)

* To die is a universal law.

Publilius Syrus, *Sententiae*. (c. 43 B.C.)

* Tutti moriremo.

Scritti apocrifi: Ecclesiastico, 8:7. Edizioni Paoline

We all must die.

Apocrypha: Ecclesiasticus, 8:7. Revised Standard Version - Catholic Edition

* Ieri a me e oggi a te.

Scritti apocrifi, Ecclesiastico, 38:23. Garzanti

Yesterday for me, and to day for thee.

Apocrypha: Ecclesiasticus, 38:23. Douay Version

* All men are fated to die.

Sophocles, *Electra*, 1. 860. (c. 413 B.C.)

* All men must die.
    Pindar, *Olympian Odes*, ode 1, 1. 82. (c. 475 B.C.)

228. *Tutto ha una fine.*

Everything has an end.
    John Ray, *English Proverbs*. (1670)

* Everything has an end, and a pudding has two.
    Thomas Nashe, *Four Letters Confuted*, p. 28. (1592)

* Every thing hath ende.
    Geoffrey Chaucer, *The Legend of Good Women: Cleopatra*, 1. 72. (c. 1386)

* Man is accomodated to life, not given to him.
    Publilius Syrus, *Sententiae*. (c. 43 B.C.)

* Il Signore ha dato, il Signore ha tolto.
    Antico Testamento: Giobbe, 1:21. Diodati, tr.

The Lord gave, and the Lord hath taken away.
    Old Testament: Job, 1:21. King James Version

229. *Ogni dì vien sera.*

* Non vien di che non venga sera.

Every day has its night.
    An English proverb

* The morning sun never lasts a day.
    John Ray, *English Proverbs*. (1678)

* The longest day must have an end.
    John Ray, *English Proverbs*. (1670)

* Be the day never so long,

Evermore at last they ring to evensong.
    John Heywood, *Proverbs*, pt. II, ch. 7. (1546)

230. *Tutti i fiumi vanno al mare.*

* Ogni acqua va al mare.

All rivers run into the sea.
    Thomas Draxe, *Bibliotheca*. (1616)

* L'acqua va al mare.
    John Florio, *Firste Fruites*. (1578)

The water goes to the sea.

Florio, *ibid.*

* Tutti i fiumi corrono al mare.

  Antico Testamento: Ecclesiaste, 1:7. Garzanti

All rivers run into the sea.

  Old Testament: Ecclesiastes, 1:7. King James Version

231. *Tutti siamo nati per morire.*

(We were all born to die).

* Our birth is nothing but our death begun.

  Edward Young, *Night Thoughts*: Night V, 1. 717. (1742)

* Born but to die.

  Alexander Pope, *An Essay on Man*: Epistle 11,1. 10. (1734)

* The first breath is the beginning of death.

  Thomas Fuller, *Gnomologia.* (1732)

* He that is born once, once must die.

  George Herbert, *Jacula Prudentum.* (1651)

* What then remains but that we still should cry

For being born, and, being born, to.die?

  Francis Bacon, *The World.* (c. 1628)

* All that live must die,

Passing. through nature to eternity.

  Shakespeare, *Hamlet*, act I, sc. ii, 1. 72. (1600)

* We were born to die.

  Shakespeare, *Romeo and Juliet*, act III, sc. iv, 1. 4. (1595)

* We are born to die.

  George Pettie, *Petite Pallace*, p. 49. (1576)

* The whole life is nothing but a journey to death.

  Seneca, *Ad Polybium De Consolatione*, ch. 11, sec. 2. (c. A.D. 64)

* As soon as we are born we begin to die.

  Marcus Manilius, *Astronomica*, bk. IV, ch. 16. (c. 15 B.C.)

232. *Come si vive, così si muore.*

* Dimmi la vita che fai e ti dirò la morte che farai.

As we live so shall we die.

  Mario Hazon, *Grande Dizionario Inglese - Italiano, Italiano- Inglese.* (1974)

* This human life is best understood by the wise man's rule,
of regarding the end.

   Jonathan Swift, *A Tale of a Tub*. sec. 7. (1704)

* As a man lives so shall he die,

As a tree falls so shall it lie.

   John Ray, *English Proverbs*. (1670)

* Such a life, such a death.

   John Clarke, *Paroemiologia*. (1639)

* Qual vita, tal fine.

   John Florio, *Firste Fruites*. (1578)

Such a life, such an end.

   Florio, *ibid*.

* The end depends upon the beginning.

   Marcus Manilius, *Astronomica*, bk. IV, ch. 16. (c. 15 B.C.)

* L'albero ove cade ivi resta.

   Antico Testamento: Ecclesiaste, 11:3. Garzanti

Where the tree falleth, there it shall be.

   Old Testaments Ecclesiastes, 11:3. King James Version

233. Chi ben vive, ben muore.

   John Florio, *Firste Fruites*. (1578)

Who lives well, dies well.

   Florio, *ibid*.

* It matters not how long we live, but how.

   Philip James Bailey, *Festus: Wood and Water*. (1839)

* Nor love thy life, nor hate; but what thou liv'st

Live well; how long, or short, permit to Heaven.

   John Milton, *Paradise Lost:*.bk. XI, 1. 553. (1667)

* They die well that live well.

   John Clarke, *Paroemiologia*. (1639)

* A good life will have a good end.

   Thomas Draxe, *Bibliotheca*. (1616)

* Live righteously, you will die righteously.

   Ovid, *Amores*, bk. III, elegy 9, 1. 37. (c. 13 B.C.)

* He that lives well, shall die well.

Attributed to Socrates. (c. 400 B.C.)

* Wouldst thou learn to die well? Learn first to live well.

Confucius. (c. 500 B.C.) From William Gowan, *The Phenix: Morals of Confucius.*

234. *Tanto è morir di male quanto d'amore.*

It is all one whether you die of sickness or of love.

Henry George Bohn, *Handbook of Proverbs.* (1855)

* Charon waits for all.

Thomas Fuller, *Gnomologia.* (1732)

* All that wear feathers first or last

Must one day perch on Charon's mast.

Matthew Prior, *Turtle and Sparrow.* (1708)

* We inn diversely, but end alike.

John Clarke, *Paroemiologia.* (1639)

* We all die alike, even though our doom is diverse.

Pindar, *Isthmian Odes*, ode 7, 1.42. (c. 456 B.C.)

235. *E'meglio morir con onore che con vergogna.*

(It's better to die with honor than with shame).

* A fair death honors the whole life.

George Herbert, *Jacula Prudentum.* (1640)

* It is far better to die with honor than to live with shame.

John Florio, *Firste Fruites.* (1578)

* Un bel morir tutta la vita onora.

(A good death honors the whole life)

Francesco Petrarca, *Il Canzoniere*, canzone XX, stanza 5. (c. 1348)

* An honorable death is better than a disgraceful life.

Tacitus, *Agricola*, sec. 33. (c. A.D. 98)

* An honorable death is preferable to a disgraceful life.

Publilius Syrus, *Sententiae.* (c. 43 B.C.)

236. *La morte non guarda calendario.*

Death keeps no Calendar.

George Herbert, *Jacula Prudentum.* (1640)

* The doors of death are ever open.

Bishop Jeremy Taylor, *Contemplation on the State of Man*, bk. I, ch. 7. (c. 1660)

* L'uomo non conosce la sua ora

    Antico Testamento: Ecclesiaste, 9:12. Garzanti

Man knoweth not his time.

    Old Testament: Ecclesiastes, 9:12. King James Version

237. *La morte viene quando meno s'aspetta.*

(Death comes when least expected)

* Death surprises us in the midst of our hopes.

    Thomas Fuller, *Gnomologia*. (1732)

* Deaths foreseen come not.

    George Herbert, *Jacula Prudentum*. (1640)

* Death has a thousand doors to let out life.

    Philip Massinger *A Very Woman*, act V, sc. iv. (1630)

* In the midst of life we are in death.

    The Book of Common Prayer: Burial of the Dead: at the Grave.

* It is uncertain where death may be waiting for you,
therefore expect it everywhere.

    Seneca, *Ad Lucilium*, epistle XXVI, sec. 7. (c. A.D. 64)

* We must once die, but not when we will.

    Publilius Syrus, *Sententiae*. (c. 43 B.C.)

238. *La morte è di casa Nonsisà. (Toscano)*

(No one knows where death is).

* Death meets us everywhere.

    Thomas Fuller, *Gnomologia*. (1732)

* E apparve un cavallo verdastro, il cui cavaliere aveva nome Morte.

    Nuovo Testamento: Apocalisse, 6:8. Garzanti

And behold a pale horses and his name that sat on him was Death.

    New Testament: Revelation, 6:8. King James Version

* Death is everywhere.

    Seneca, *Phoenissae*, 1. 151. (c. A.D. 60)

239. *La morte non riceve alcuna scusa.*

(Death accepts no excuses)

* Death is deaf and will hear no denial.

    An English proverb

* Death's a debt; his mandamus binds all alike - no bail, no demurrer.

Richard Brinsley Sheridan, *St. Patrick's Day*, act II, sc. iv. (1775)

* Death takes no bribes.

Benjamin Franklin, *Poor Richard's Almanack*. (1742)

* Death is deaf.

Miguel de Cervantes, *Don Quixote de la Mancha*, pt. II, ch. 7. (1615)

* We owe God a death.

Shakespeare, *King Henry IV*, Part II, act III, sc. ii, 1. 250. (1598)

* Death takes no denial.

Euripides, *The Bacchae*, 1. 1002. (c. 407 B.C.)

* Death is a debt which all of.us must pay.

Sophocles, *Electra*, 1. 1173. (c. 413 B.C.)

240. *Contro la morte non v'è cosa forte.*

(Nothing is stronger than death).

* There is no king more terrible than death.

Henry Austin Dobson, *The Dance of Death*. (1877)

* There is no god found stronger than death.

Algernon Charles Swinburne, *Hymn to Proserpine*. (1866)

* Death defies the doctor.

James Kelly, *Scottish Proverbs*. (1721)

* Death will seize the doctor too.

Shakespeare, *Cymbeline*, act V, sc. v, 1. 29. (1609)

* Wheresoever ye be, death will overtake you,

although ye be in lofty towers.

Mohammed, *The Koran*, ch. 4. (c. A.D. 622) George Sale, tr.

* Il re dei terrori.

Antico Testamento: Giobbe, 18,14. Edizioni Paoline

The king *of* terrors.

Old Testament: Job, 18:14. King James Version

241. *La morte non sparagna re di Francia né di Spagna*

(Death spares neither the king of France nor of Spain)

* Inexorable death, who was never known to respect merit.

Benjamin Franklin, *Poor Richard's Almanack*. (1733)

* Death lays his icy hand on kings.

James Shirley, *The Contention of Ajax and Ulysses*, sc. iii. (1659)

* Death, as the Psalmist saith, is certain to all; all shall die.

  Shakespeare, *King Henry IV*, Part II, act III, sc. ii, 1. 41. (1598)

* Chi è re oggi, domani finirà.

  Scritti apocrifi: Ecclesiastico, 10:10. Garzanti

He that is today a king tomorrow shall die.

  Apocrypha: Ecclesiasticus, 10:10. American Bible Society

* Voi siete dei ... Eppure morrete, come semplici mortali,
e come uno dei principi comuni, crollerete.

  Antico Testamento: Salmi, 82:6-7. Garzanti

Ye are gods ... But ye shall die like men,
and fall like one of the princes.

  Old Testament: Psalms, 82:6-7. King James Version

242. *La morte pareggia tutti.*

(Death makes all equal)

* Death takes both the weak and the strong.

  Benjamin Franklin, *Poor Richard's Almanack*. (1737)

* The end makes all equal.

  Thomas Fuller, *Gnomologia*. (1732)

* Death is the grand leveller.

  Thomas Fuller, *Gnomologia*. (1732)

* Death makes equal the high and low.

  John Heywood, *Be Merry. Friends*. (c. 1546)

* Pale Death ... knocks at the poor man's cottage door
and at the palaces of kings.

  Horace, *Odes*, bk. I, ode iv, 1. 13. (c. 23 B.C.)

* Tutto viene dalla polvere e tutto torna in polvere.

  Antico Testamento: Ecclesiaste, 3:20. Garzanti

All are of dust, and all turn to dust again.

  Old Testament: Ecclesiastes, 3:20. King James James Version

Tu sei polvere e in polvere ritornerai.

  Antico Testamento: Genesi, 3:19. Edizioni Paoline

Dust thou art, and unto dust shalt thou return.

  Old Testament: Genesis, 3:19 King James Version

243. *La morte altro non è che un eterno sonno.*

John Florio. *Firste Fruites*. (1578)

Death is nought else but an eternal sleep.

Florio, *ibid.*

* Death is a sleep.

Algernon Charles Swinburne, *Hymn to Proserpine*. (1866)

* Death is an eternal sleep.

Joseph Fouché, Inscription. (1794) As French Minister of Police, he had the inscription placed on the gates of all French cemeteries.

* Death rock me asleep.

Shakespeare, *King Henry IV*, Part II, act II, sc. iv, 1. 211. (1598)

* The eternal sleep.

Horace, *Odes*. bk. I, ode xxiv. 1. 5. (c. 23 B.C.)

244. *Il sonno è parente della morte.*

(Sleep is closely related to death).

* Sleep, Death's twin brother.

Lord Tennyson, *In Memoriam*, pt. LXVIII, stanza 1. (1850)

* How wonderful is Death,

Death and his brother Sleep!

Percy Bysshe Shelley, *Queen Mab*, pt. I, 1. 1. (1813)

* Sleep is the image of death.

John Clarke, *Paroemiologia*. (1639)

* O sleep. thou ape of death.

Shakespeare, *Cymbeline*, act II, sc. ii, 1. 31. (1609)

* Sleep ... brother to death.

Samuel Daniel, *Sonnets to Delia*. (1592)

* Dal sonno a la Morte è un picciol varco.

(Sleep is very close to death).

Torquato Tasso, *La Gerusalemme Liberata*, canto IX, stanza 18. (1581)

* Death's own brother, Sleep.

Virgil, *Aeneid*, bk. VI, 1. 278. (c. *19* B.C.)

* Sleep, brother to Death.

Homer. *Iliad*. bk. XIV. 1.231. (c. 850 B.C.)

245. *I morti e gli andati son presto dimenticati.*

The dead are soon forgotten.

An English proverb

* He that died half year ago is as dead as Adam.
    Thomas Fuller. *Gnomologia*. (1732)

* The dead ... are forgotten.
    Thomas Fuller, *Church History of Britain*, pt. IX, bk. iv, ch. 3. (1655)

* He is dead and gone, lady,

He is dead and gone.
    Shakespeare. *Hamlet*, act IV, sc. v.I. 29. (1600)

* Io sono stato dimenticato dal cuor loro come un morto.
    Antico Testamento: Salmi, 31:12. Diodati. tr.

I am forgotten as a dead man out of mind.
    Old Testament: Psalms, 31:12. King James Version

* The dead are dead.
    Euripides, *Alcestis*, 1. 541. (c. 438 B.C.)

* Egli non ritornerà più a casa sua,

e il luogo suo non lo riconoscerà più.
    Antico Testamento: Giobbe, 7:10. Diodati, tr.

He shall return no more to his house,

neither shall his place know him any more.
    Old Testament: Job, 7:10. King James Version

246. *Chi muore giace e chi vive si dà pace.*

* I morti testa a testa, e i vivi fanno festa. (Calabrese)

* I morti con i morti, e i vivi con i vivi. (Napoletano)

(He who dies lies, and he who lives sets his mind at rest).

* Let the dead bury the dead.
    Mario Hazon, *Grande Dizionario Inglese-Italiano, Italiano-Inglese*. (1974)

* "Cloth must we wear,

Eat beef and drink beer,

Though the dead go to bier."
    Sir Walter Scott, *The Betrothed*, ch. 10 (1825)

* The earth belongs to the living. not to the dead.
    Thomas Jefferson, *Letter to John W. Eppes*. June 24, 1813.

* To the grave with the dead;

And let them that live, to the bread.

Thomas Fuller, *Gnomologia*. (1732)

* The dead to the grave and the living to the loaf.

Miguel de Cervantes. *Don Quixote de la Mancha*, pt. I, ch. 19. (1605)

* Vivi con vivi. e morti con morti.

John Florio, *Firste Fruites*. (1578)

Quick with the quick, and dead with the dead.

Florio, *ibid.*

* Lascia che i morti seppelliscano i loro morti.

Nuovo Testamento: Matteo, 8:22. Edizioni Paoline

Let the dead bury their dead.

New Testament: Matthew, 8:22. King James Version

247. *Generazione che va, generazione che viene, ma la terra rimane sempre.*

Antico Testamento: Ecclesiaste, 1:4. Edizioni Paoline

One generation passeth away, and another generation cometh:
but the earth abideth for ever.

Old Testament: Ecclesiastes, 1:4. King James Version

* Every minute dies a man,

Every minute one is born.

Lord Tennyson, *The Vision of Sin*, pt. IV, stanza 9. (1842)

* Some laugh, while others mourn;

Some toil, while others pray;

One dies, and one is born;

So runs the world away.

Samuel Wesley, *Way of the World*. (1685)

* Some come, some go;

This life is so.

Thomas Tusser, *Five Hundred Points of Good Husbandry: August's Abstract*. (1573)

* Come foglie spuntate su albero frondoso,

che l'una cade e l'altra sboccia,

così sono le generazioni umane;

una muore e l'altra nasce.

Scritti apocrifi, Ecclesiastico, 14:18. Edizioni Paoline

As of the green leaves on a thick tree,

some fall, and some grow,

so is the generation of flesh and blood,

one cometh to an end, and another is born.

Apocrypha: Ecclesiasticus, 14:18. American Bible Society

* Life in this universe never stops and continues forever -

that is God's law.

Confucius, *The Analects*. (c. 500 B.C.) From Lin Yutang, *The Wisdom of Confucius*.

PROVERBI ITALIANI
ITALIAN PROVERBS

A

B

C

D

L

M

T

U

V

PROVERBI INGLESI
ENGLISH PROVERBS

A

151

154

I

K

L

O

P

W

Y

Indice degli autori/
Index of Authors

A

Addison, Joseph (1672-1719), 43
Aeschylus, (525-456 B.C.), 53, 76, 96, 120
Aesop (c. 620- c. 560 B.C.), 83, 91
Aiken, Conrad Potter (1889-1973), 16
Alighieri, see Dante Alighieri
Anonymous,
       Ballads, 25
       Book of Meery Riddles,(1629), 94
       Nursery Rhymes, 31
Proverbs
       Chinese, 84, 103
       Dutch, 114, 124
       English, 11, 12, 21-3, 25, 26, 31, 33-4, 44-5, 48, 54, 57, 63-4, 69, 71, 81, 83-4, 93, 99, 103, 105, 107-9, 114, 126, 130, 134
       Flemish, 81
       French, 41
       Gaelic, 63, 120
       German, 33, 83, 97, 98, 99
       Icelandic, 54
       Latin, 15, 33, 71, 75, 86, 102, 106-7, 114, 124
       Scottish , 11, 19
       Scottish jingle, 39

Apuleius (c. A.D. 125-c.180), 31
Arbuthnot, John (1667-1735), 52
Ariosto, Ludovico (1474-1533), 121
Aristophanes (c. 448- c. 380 B.C.), 43
Aristotle (384-322 B.C.),   64
Arnold, Sir Edwin (1832-1904), 115, 121
Arouet, F. M., see Voltaire
Aurelius, Marcus (c. 121 A.D.-180 A.D.), 115, 120
Austin, Alfred (1835-1913), 111

B

Bacon, Francis (1561-1626), 65, 70, 83, 107, 116, 123, 127
Bailey, Nathan (?-1742), 23
Bailey, Philip James (1816-1902), 128
Barclay, Alexander (c. 1475-1552), 14
Barnfield, Richard (1574-1627), 16
Barrie, James Matthew (1860-1937), 28, 73

Brooke, Rupert (1887-1915), 105
Browning, Elizabeth Barrett (1806-1861), 17, 42, 61,
Browning, Robert (1812-1889), 28, 117
Bunyan, John (1628-1688), 103
Burgess, Gelett (1866-1951), 48
Burns, Robert (1759-1796), 33
Burton, Robert (1577-1640), 24, 37, 46, 63, 66, 68-70, 74, 82
Butler, Samuel (1835-1902), 28
Butler, Samuel (1612-1680), 28, 83, 90
Byron, George Gordon, Lord (1788-1824), 21, 50, 69, 76-7, 100-1, 110, 123

C

Calderon de la Barca, Pedro (1600-1681), 117
Carducci, Giosuè (1835-1907), 117
Carew, Thomas (c. 1595-c. 1645), 26
Caterina da Siena, Santa (1347-1380), 116
Cato, Marcus Porcius, the Elder, (234-149 B.C.), 46
Catullus, Gaius Valerius (c.87- 54 B.C.), 99
Cavendish, Margaret see Newcastle, Duchess of
Cervantes, Miguel de (1547-1616), 12, 36, 39, 44, 69, 96, 114, 131, 135
Chapman, George (c. 1559-1634), 44, 86
Chaucer, Geoffrey (c. 1343-1400), 14, 20, 23, 47, 70, 84, 85, 102, 104-5, 115,
    120, 126
Christie, Agatha (1890-1976), 28, 75
Cibber, Colley (1671-1757), 43, 70
Cicero, Marcus Tullius (106-43 B.C.), 13, 53, 56, 61, 66, 81, 96, 97, 104, 124
Clarke, John (fl. 1639), 12, 14, 21, 30, 45, 58, 65, 75, 87, 90, 98, 101, 102, 104,
    107, 128, 129, 133
Clemens. Samuel Langhorne, see Twain, Mark
Cobb, Will D. (1876-1930), 12
Coke, Sir Edward (1552-1634), 54
Coleridge, Samuel Taylor (1772-1834), 15, 82
Collins, Mortimer (1827-1876), 48
Combe, William (1741-1823), 55
Confucius, (551-478 B.C.), 32, 74, 129, 136
Congreve, William (1670-1729), 28, 65, 67, 77, 95
Corneille, Pierre (1606-1684), 24
Cotgrave, Randle (?-1634), 29, 51-2, 54, 56, 58, 86, 110
Crabbe, George (1754-1832), 28
Craik, Dinah Maria Mulock (1826-1887), 108

D

Daniel, Samuel (1562-1619), 48, 110, 133
Dante Alighieri, (1265-1321), 17, 22, 26, 84, 105, 122
Davies, John, of Hereford, (c. 1565-1618), 33, 54, 62, 94, 98
Defoe, Daniel (c.1661-1731), 121, 123

Dekker, Thomas (1572-1632), 17, 46, 68, 78, 108, 110
Denham, Sir John (1615-1669), 88
Dickens, Charles (1812-1870), 24, 25, 54
Diogenes, the Cynic (c. 400- 325 B.C.), 65
Disraeli, Benjamin (1804-1881), 61
Dobson, Henry Austin (1840-1921), 40, 131
Doolittle, Justus (fl. 1872) , 84
Draxe, Thomas (?-1618), 13, 17, 19, 31, 34, 64, 66, 69, 86, 94, 99, 116, 128
Dryden, John (1631-1700), 11, 13, 16, 27, 37, 80, 95, 96, 103
D'Urfey, Thomas (1653-1723), 95

E

Eliot,Thomas Stearns (1888-1965) , 53
Emerson, Ralph Waldo (1803-1882), 20, 35, 36, 38, 54, 69, 93, 96, 99, 102, 105-
    6, 114, 116
Etienne, Charles Guillaume (1778-1845), 26
Euripides, (c. 480-406 B.C.), 30, 35, 43, 49, 68, 77, 93, 99, 114-5, 121-2, 131,
    134

F

Farquhar, George (1678-1707), 69, 80
Ferguson, David (1532-1598), 21, 64, 77, 79, 85, 120
Field, Nathaniel (1587-1633), 44
Fielding, Thomas (fl.1824), 51
Fletcher, John (1579-1625), 45, 68, 70, 107
Fletcher, Phineas (1582-1650), 13
Florio, John (1553-1625), 11, 16, 21, 23, 25, 32, 37, 41, 45, 48-49, 57, 59, 62, 66,
    70, 77, 94-5, 103, 107, 114, 118, 126, 128-9, 133, 135
Ford, John (1586-1639), 40
Ford, Lena Guilbert (?- 1915), 105
Fouché, Joseph (1763-1820), 133
France, Anatole (Jacques Anatole Francois Thibault), (1844-1924), 40
Franklin, Benjamin (1706-1790), 14, 23-4, 28, 32-5, 44, 51, 56, 58, 61-2, 64-66,
    70, 74, 77, 80, 90, 97, 102, 113, 124, 131-2
Frost, Robert (1874-1963) , 57
Fuller, Thomas (1608-1661), 11-2, 15-6, 21, 23, 26, 29, 32-6, 39-40, 44-5, 51, 56,
    58, 62, 64-5, 67, 71, 73-6, 80, 82-3, 85-8, 90, 93, 97-8, 103-4, 107-110, 115,
    119, 121, 123-4, 127, 129-30, 132, 134-5

G

Galt, John (1779-1839), 29
Garrick, David (1716-1779), 76, 102
Gay, John (1688-1732), 14, 50, 82
Gilbert, William Schwenck (1836-1911), 22, 40, 84, 105
Glyde, John Jr., (fl. 1872), 85
Goethe, Johann Wolfgang von (1749-1832) 37, 40, 41, 101
Gogol Nikolai (1809-1852), 101

Jerome, St. (c. A.D. 340-420), 22
Jerrold, Douglas William (1803-1857), 97
Johnson, Samuel (1709-1784), 61, 98
Jonson, Ben (1572-1637) 68, 95
Juvenal, Decimus (c. A.D. 50- 140) 121

K

Keats, John (1795-1821) 29, 53
Kelly, James (fl 1721), 15, 23, 25, 42, 49, 51, 56, 58, 59, 65, 69, 73-7, 80, 86, 87,
    88, 102, 120, 131
Kin, David (no data), 93
Kingsley, Charles (1819-1875), 110
Knowles, James Sheridan (1784-1862), 14
Koran, The, see Mohammed

L

La Fontaine, Jean de (1621-1695), 29, 122
Lamb, Charles (1775-1834), 125
La Rochefoucauld, Francois, Duc de (1613-1680), 16, 18, 24
Lessing, Gotthold Ephraim (1729-1781), 43
L'Estrange, Sir Roger (1616-1704), 48
Livy, Titus Livius (59 B.C.-A.D. 17), 119
Lodge, Thomas (c. 1558-1625), 36
Logan, John (c. 1748-1788), 95
Longfellow, Henry Wadsworth (1807-1882) 19, 55, 116-9
Lucretius, Titus Lucretius Carus (c. 99- 55 B.C.), 101, 107
Luther, Martin (1483-1546), 50
Lyly, John (c. 1554-1606), 18, 22, 24, 27, 31-2, 34, 40, 41, 52, 69, 75, 89, 102-3,
    109

M

Malory, Sir Thomas (c. 1430-c. 1471), 27
Manilius, Marcus (c. 15 B.C), 127-8
Manningham, John (?-1622), 52, 71
Marcus Aurelius Antoninus , see Aurelius Marcus
Marlowe, Christopher (1564-1593), 25, 120
Marryat, Frederick (1792-1848), 125
Martial (Marcus Valerius Martialis) (A.D. c. 40-c 104), 102
Masefield, John (1878-1967), 102
Massinger, Philip (1583-1640), 31, 54, 67, 82, 130
McGlennon, Felix (1856-1943), 55
Menander, (c. 342-292 B.C.), 24, 65, 66, 81, 83, 123
Meurier, Gabriel (c. 1530-1601), 27, 46, 47
Middleton, Thomas (1580-1627), 57, 63, 67, 122
Mill, John Stuart (1806-1873), 98
Miller, Joaquin (Cincinnatus Hiner), (c. 1841-1913), 106
Milton, John (1608-1674), 24, 49, 88, 128

Punch, (1845), 65

Taylor, Sir Henry (1800-1886), 86
Tennyson, Alfred, Lord (1809-1892), 21, 28, 42, 74, 104-5, 133, 135
Terence, Publius Terentius Afer (c. 190-159 B.C.), 24, 29
Thackeray, William Makepeace (1811-1863), 50, 89
Thales (c. 640-546 B.C.), 65
Themistocles (c. 528-c.462 B.C.), 89
Thibault, Jacques, See France, Anatole
Thoreau, Henry David (1817-1862), 35-6, 98, 109, 116, 118
Tolstoy, Leo Nikolaevich (1828-1910), 35, 82
Trench, Richard Chenevix (1807-1886), 12
Truman, Harry S. (1884-1972), 114
Tusser, Thomas (c. 1524-1580), 56, 57, 135
Twain, Mark (Samuel Langhorne Clemens), (1835-1910), 81, 89, 99, 109

V

Vanbrugh, Sir John (1664-1726), 43, 75
Venning, Ralph (1621-1674), 33, 90
Virgil, (Publius Virgilius Maro) (70-19B.C.), 18, 21, 23, 43, 115, 121, 133
Voltaire (François Marie Arouet), (1694-1778), 11, 35
Voss, Johann Heinrich (1751-1826), 50

W

Wallace, Lew (1827-1905), 35
Watson, Thomas (c. 1557-1592), 17
Watts, Isaac (1674-1748), 115
Webster, John (1580-1625), 46, 67
Wentworth, Patricia (1878-1961), 23, 109
Wesley, Samuel (1662-1735), 135
White, Edward (1819-1898), 15
Whyte-Melville, George John (1821-1878), 39, 85
Wilcox, Ella Wheeler (1850-1919), 100, 106
Wilde, Oscar Fingal (1854-1900), 27, 38, 63, 66
Wilkins, George (fl. 1607), 47
Wodroephe, John (fl. 1623), 37
Wolcot, John, see Pindar, Peter
Wordsworth, William (1770-1850), 88, 123
Wotton, Sir Henry (1568-1639), 41

Y

Yeats, William Butler (1865-1939), 12, 33
Young, Edward (1683-1765), 69, 127

MEMBER OF SCABRINI MEDIA

Quebec, Canada
2004